Michael Caine

The role that changed Michael Caine's life, as the junior lieutenant in Zulu.

Michael Caine

PHILIP JUDGE

SPELLMOUNT LTD
Tunbridge Wells, Kent

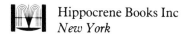

Hippocrene Books Inc
New York

For my family
For my friends
And for the good times

First published in the UK in 1985 by
SPELLMOUNT LTD
12 Dene Way, Speldhurst
Tunbridge Wells, Kent TN3 ONX

ISBN 0-946771-41-3 (UK)

British Library Cataloguing in Publication Date
Judge, Philip
Michael Caine. – (Film and Theatre Stars)
1. Caine, Michael 2. Actors –
United States – Biography
1. Title 2. Series

First published in USA 1985 by
HIPPOCRENE BOOKS INC.
171 Madison Avenue
New York, NY 10016

ISBN 0-87052-124-1 (USA)

Commissioning Editor: Sue Rolfe
Design: Sue Ryall

Printed & bound in Great Britain
by Biddles Ltd, Guilford, Surrey.

Contents

Acknowledgements and thanks are due to the following for the reproduction of the pictures:

Cinema International Corporation: 1, 9-11; The Author: 2-5, 22, 26-8, 31, 33, 34, 38-40, 42; BBC Television: 6-8; National Film Archive: 12-14, 29-30, 32; Paramount CIC: 15-17, 18-20, 23-4; Associated Press: 21; United Artists: 25; Universal Pictorial Press Photos: 35; Columbia-EMI-Warner Distribution Ltd: 36, 37; Jenny Agutter/Woman's Own: 41.

List of Illustrations

Prologue

June, 1984. St. Lucia. 2 a.m.

Michael Caine sat on the verandah of the Halcyon Days Hotel, staring out at the lights of the fishing boats sparkling like scattered jewels on the dark waters of Marigo Bay far below. A propellor blade in the ceiling above him lazily stirred the sluggish air.

The warm southerly wind turned the surface of the sea into wrinkled black skin. The rhythm of a steel band floated up from somewhere along the beach. It was a still, balmy night and the soft billow of surf sending its phosphoresence into the air to play hide and seek with the fire-flies was like distant thunder.

Caine drew on the soggy remnants of what had once been a hand-rolled eight-inch Havana cigar, sipped more red wine, and sighed with deep satisfaction. They had beaten the rainy season by a week. Yet another exotic location was almost through, he had relished every minute of it, and soon they would be heading back to England for the final scenes on the wild comedy called simply *Water* in Shepperton Studios and in glorious summertime Devon. Caine would be home, where his roots are.

He started to tick off names on the fingers of one big hand, counting them aloud. 'Zululand . . . the Deep South . . . Finland — never again . . . the Philippines . . . Almeria — what a dump! Oh yeah, don't forget Austria, Berlin, Budapest, Majorca . . . and we haven't even touched the South of France, Pinewood and Hollywood.'

He smiled quietly, and said: 'Y'know, I can pick up a script now and if it begins: *"It's midwinter. Our hero is stumbling through the snow in northern Alaska with his dog sleigh"* — I shut it up again, quick! I've reached that point in my life where I can pick and choose what I want.

'There were times when I thought it would never happen. So now that it *has* happened, and I'm here, I sit back like this sometimes and I think: *it can't be bad, can it?*' No, not bad at all.

I have watched Michael Caine facing the cameras across the world, and it is fascinating to see him at work.

Always there has been one outstanding factor present: a stillness about him — watchful, almost wary — acting as a rock of reassurance when all around him the floodwaters of potential panic, conflicting tempers and near-hysteria swirl and churn as they can do on any film set.

It is a stillness born of years of patience. Here is a man who played the waiting game for so long that practically nothing can rattle him any more.

I was present at the critical moment when the spotlight finally wavered his way, focused — and stayed firmly fixed on the tall man with the curly fair hair, big hands, unmistakable voice and horn-rimmed spectacles. It was the moment when Michael Caine's life changed from being a nobody into a somebody. He made sure it never eluded him again.

The film was the epic *Zulu*. Caine had been hanging around in the wings long enough, waiting for the call. As he said to me recently: *'I've been thirty years a loser, twenty years a winner'*.

Today the winning years are rapidly overhauling the losers. And, once you know Michael Caine's story, can you begrudge him his success?

Chapter 1
Early Days

Who could have guessed it on that squally Tuesday morning on March 14, 1933, when Mrs Ellen Micklewhite was admitted to St Olave's Hospital, Rotherhithe, to give birth to her first child, an 8lb 2oz baby boy? He was christened Maurice Joseph Micklewhite, following the tradition of three centuries, when all the first-born boys in the Micklewhite family were called Maurice.

Caine used to say much later: 'When you're born a Cockney, there's no way to go but up'. But he has remained fiercely loyal to his humble beginnings to this day.

He was born a Cockney — just. If the wind blows hard enough across the River Thames, it could conceivably have carried the sound of Bow Bells over the wharves and rooftops of Limehouse and into Victoria Ward on the first floor of St Olave's, to echo Maurice's first cries in that hard world of the thirties depression.

Besides which, Ellen came from stout East End stock, a small sturdy Cockney soul herself who had been a charwoman all her life. His father Maurice, senior, tried to follow two generations of Micklewhites into the fish trade. But in that cruel era he was one of the victims of the gigantic Depression — part of the 'irreducible million', a grim statistic which meant that between the two world wars unemployment never fell below that level. Only now it stood at over three million, and Maurice Senior was just another lined face in the dole queue around the corner from their shabby home off the Old Kent Road.

The young Michael Caine grew up against a background of poverty etched in the faces of the grey men in mufflers who trudged the hard pavements of South London searching for work. His mother scrubbed steps and sewed buttons at a local clothing shop for ten shillings a week to survive.

They existed like that for two years, and Michael would hear about it much later from his 'old lady': how, for example, his father would come home and slump into his faded leather armchair in the kitchen with a bottle of beer for the evening, to stare through the window at the grimy rooftops outside for hours on end without speaking.

When he was six months old the family was summarily moved out of the Old Kent Road by the local council. The place was to be torn down as part of a slum clearance project. They were rehoused in a dilapidated Victorian house in Camberwell, which became their home for the next six years; they occupied the middle floor, just two rooms, and shared the yellow-brick house with three other families.

Caine recalls: 'One room was a living-room and kitchen combined. I remember an old stove in it that my mother was always black-leading. The other was the bedroom, and all of us slept there'.

'All of us' would soon include his baby brother Stanley, born three years later, who moved into the cot while Michael was elevated to a small bed.

The tough backstreets of South London became his playground, and inevitably a battleground too. At school, his long blond curls and innocent blue eyes brought the unwilling recipient the immediate nickname of 'Teacher's pet'. Caine remembers it all too well, his first verbal and physical scars in the endurance test of life.

'I was always in trouble. I was the kind of kid who looked like Little Lord Fauntleroy — except for my expression. That didn't go with the hair at all!' Many evenings he would arrive home with a swollen nose and grazed knees from playground fights. If young Maurice lacked anything, it wasn't the courage to stand up for himself.

'My father taught me a lot about survival,' he says. 'He was an extraordinarily strong man, very big and tough without an ounce of fat on him. Being a Billingsgate fish porter builds up the muscles. It's not exactly a sedentary job.' Mr Micklewhite passed on that instinct for survival to his son, imbuing him with a wit, shrewdness and pungent humour that would prove vital for his welfare on the hard uphill road that lay ahead.

12

His father proved to be a dominating influence in Caine's life, one that has extended through to this day. When Maurice Senior finally found regular work in the fish market, he immediately demanded that his wife gave up her job and reserved her energies for keeping the family intact, fed and clothed. 'He always regarded himself as the breadwinner. He had very fixed ideas,' says Caine. 'He'd do all the heavy work like lugging up coal from the cellar. But he wouldn't even wash a tea-cup. That was a woman's job.'

Caine still goes along with this way of thinking. It hardly endears him to feminists, but for many women forms part of his innate attraction. Male chauvinist he may be — but they see a challenge there, too.

In those days the young Maurice would get up at 4 am in his school holidays and trot off to the market to help his father in the early light of dawn. Small and vociferous, the curly-haired kid would stand by as his dad hammered the lids on fish boxes he had freshly iced, offering advice and encouragement.

The war split the family in two. Mr Micklewhite was with the British Expeditionary Force at Dunkirk, and later joined the Eighth Army for the vital push up through Sicily and Italy. He came home with a corporal's stripes on his arm.

Ellen Micklewhite took young Maurice and Stanley to the comparative safety of North Runcton (pop 280) in Norfolk, where they settled into a rambling old farmhouse next to the village school with five other London evacuee families. For six happy years Caine forgot the grime and poverty of South London, and found a 'magic time' amid the fresh air, fens and endless flatlands of the Norfolk countryside.

'It was wonderful. After being hemmed in by ugly buildings and dirty brick walls I could suddenly see all the way to the horizon. I felt a tremendous sense of freedom. I wanted to run and simply keep on running . . .'

The magic time ended on VE Day, 8 May 1945. The Micklewhites sadly packed their bags and took the train home to London. Their house in Camberwell had been flattened by the Luftwaffe. They were rehoused in a 'prefab' down the road, which became their home for the next ten years.

Young Maurice took a scholarship to Hackney Downs Grocers' School, stayed a year, and at the age of thirteen won himself a place in

The young Michael Micklewhite, with his mother and father, a fish porter at Billingsgate.

Michael Caine was no sports fiend — but he did take on a girl's netball team, with his eye on the rival captain.

14

the prestigious Wilson's Grammar School near Camberwell Green. A fellow pupil at Hackney, though neither of them realised the significance, was a boy called Jerry Pam. Twenty years later he was to become Michael Caine's personal press agent, close friend and confidant, and one of the few outsiders in Caine's life to be called 'family'.

The school's motto was Non Sibi Sed Omnibus (Not for oneself, But for all), noble sentiments which could hardly have been more misplaced when it came to the aggressive young cockney rebel who joined Class 2C that September morning in 1946. From the start it was apparent that Wilson's Grammar School and Maurice Micklewhite were not going to be friends.

By now he was a tall, gangling youth with floppy fair hair and his first pair of spectacles for short-sightedness, held together with string and sticking plaster. It gave him another nickname — The Professor — but Maurice Micklewhite was no teacher's pet — if he ever had been.

It wasn't just the glasses. 'I knew a lot,' Caine says without boasting. 'I'd always been fascinated with facts, though I never passed the form tests because I couldn't do algebra or trigonometry — and maths was a basic subject.' At sixteen, his School Certificate came with English grammar, English literature, French, art, geography and history. Maths: failed.

On the field of sporting endeavour he was conspicuous by his lack of enthusiasm — and, eventually, by his absence. 'I wasn't a genius at sport,' he says today. 'The first time I played cricket I was wicket-keeper and I got hit in the unmentionables. So I gave that up. I never played cricket again because the ball was hard and I was soft! I quite liked football. I played left back, because I was big and I could stop people coming through. But I was never a lunatic sports fiend.'

Except in one direction: netball! Caine fell heavily for an attractive teenage brunette named Mary who played enthusiastic games of netball on a neighbouring court with girls from her own school. Caine, greatly enamoured, persuaded some of his cronies to form a team, and challenge them. Showing no gallantry whatsoever, they thrashed the girls 22– 3. Mary walked off in disgust and Caine never saw her again.

'I was trying to get laid for the first time,' he recalls now, a glint of wry humour behind the heavy lids. 'That's why I took it up. But I

15

never scored anything — either at netball or in the other area. You could say sport was a complete failure for me in those days, even sexually.'

That, of course, would change radically in time, but for the present young Micklewhite took refuge in his deams — and he found that the Tower Cinema in Peckham, a tempting half-mile from the school gates, was the answer to them. The Tower was the local fleapit, but it changed its programme twice a week. The Professor would hop off the bus that took the boys to the school playing fields, fork out 1s 9d, and spend the afternoon in his games kit blinking up at the screen in his own world of make-believe.

'Humphrey Bogart was my favourite actor of all time. I once wrote away for his autograph. I fouled it up because they sent me back a signed photograph, and thought the signature had been printed. So I wet my finger and rubbed it — and the ink ran all over it!'

But he admits to being 'completely besotted' by the movies. And even today he can be spotted waiting for the doors of a cinema to open at the start of a day which he will spend at the pictures. In New York where they open at 9 am, he can take in as many as six films one after the other, dashing from one cinema to another, and emerge at midnight dazed but happy. 'That's how I catch up. If I'm in Paris on my own I head straight for the Champs Elysées and do the rounds. I want to see everything.'

Marking time before his National Service, Caine was taken on as a filing clerk in the despatch department of Peak Films in Victoria, where at seventeen he earned his first wage packet: the princely sum of £3 a week. Then he was an office boy for the Wardour Street producer Jay Lewis, and had his first tantalising close-up of aspiring actors such as Richard Attenborough, Michael Medwin and Edward Judd. They never noticed him, but he took stock of them: 'I was always itching to talk to them, but I could never pluck up the courage,' he says now.

In 1951 the call came to join the army, and Private Micklewhite, M., found himself a lowly fusilier with the Queen's Royal Regiment in Germany among the Occupation forces on the Rhine. He did his best to remain inconspicuous, never volunteering for anything. 'I was the lowest form of human life, a professional private. That was the way I started, and that was the way I finished.' Except that in between he was shipped to the Korean War, to the front-line, and cowered on

16

At 17, his first job was as a filing clerk in the despatch department of a film company — his pay £2 14s. 1d. a week.

Reluctant soldier: Pte Micklewhite, M., did his National Service in the Queen's Royal Regiment, and fought in the Korean war.

17

the 38th Parallel in primitive dug-outs directly opposite the Chinese positions across the Samichon Valley. That was when warfare stopped being a game and turned into a nightmare.

During the day he dug trenches, and played cards. At night he would lie in his camp bed listening to the whine of shells overhead and wondering if he would ever escape from this hell-hole. 'It was a strange time, something outside the bounds of reality. What I remember most is the rats. The place was infested with them. Korea must have the biggest rats in the world. They'd even run over me at night when I was trying to get some sleep.'

Korea took a year out of his life. And it gave him a parting legacy: a virulent dose of malaria that caught up with him six months later — when he was on stage in a repertory theatre.

Chapter 2
What's in a name?

Like so many other young men, Michael Caine found returning home to civvy street after fighting a war was a discouraging anti-climax. No-one knew him. No-one wanted to know him. He faced a bleak, empty future with no incentives to urge him on.

He went home to his mother, and took a job in Smithfield Meat Market as a porter, less than half a mile from where his father was still labouring at Billingsgate. But somewhere along the line — perhaps it was all those hours in the half-light of the Tower at Peckham — a fuse had been lit: Michael had decided that he wanted to be an actor.

He found a copy of *The Stage*, the bible for out-of-work thespians, and ran his eye down the pages of 'job offers' and 'jobs wanted'. An assistant stage manager was required by Horsham Repertory Company in Sussex 'with occasional walk-on parts'.

Caine made for the nearest phone box and dropped four pennies in the slot. 'It was the first phone call I ever made,' he says now, with some wonderment in his voice. 'I was twenty years old. We'd never had a phone in the house, and I never had to use one before.'

But that first call struck gold — albeit a tiny vein. He was interviewed and taken on at a modest salary of £2 10s a week, which covered his board and lodging and very little else. The job meant a 14-hour day, seven days a week, and embraced such extraneous tasks as scene shifting, painting, decorating, even sweeping the stage when everyone else had left for the night. 'I was the original gopher — go for this, go for that,' Caine recalls, with a reminiscent chuckle. But he

19

was as happy as a sand-boy, because suddenly he felt he belonged somewhere.

He changed his name to Michael Scott, at the request of the management who felt that Maurice Micklewhite did not look too good on the programmes. Caine did not take offence: 'I wanted a name that was strong and short and easily identifiable.' So Michael Scott he became — and that is the name that appeared at the bottom of the cast list on his first role, playing a policeman in a mystery thriller where, just before the curtain came down, he had to march on stage to arrest the crook. He can't remember the title of the play, but he does remember vividly the moment he gripped the villain's arm and uttered the immortal words: 'Come along with me, sir!'

'It was an enormous thrill. I must have been good, because I was given that line to say in a dozen plays!' Caine had the biggest physique in the cast of fourteen — seven boys and seven girls. In fact, in his own words: 'I was built like a brick wash-house. I'd just come out of the army, so whenever they needed a tough-looking guy they came to me. I got more and more one-line parts, and eventually moved up to proper scenes.' He played butlers, waiters, Cockney ne'er-do-wells, and as the months went by the roles grew bigger in stature too.

He was on stage as Hindley Earnshaw, the weak son in *Wuthering Heights*, when 'out of the blue' he was struck down by malaria — and he fell flat on his face during the final scene. 'I just keeled over in the middle of my big speech! I don't remember a thing until I came round in the local hospital.' Finding a tiny crumb of humour in the situation, he adds: 'The woman doctor was injecting me with penicillin, and I told her it must be malaria. She said: "But you can't catch malaria in Horsham".'

In nine days his weight went down from 192 lbs to 133 lbs, and he was sent to Queen Mary's Hospital at Roehampton — where he found a dozen of his mates from the regiment, woeful faces all, in the same ward. Korea had been generous with its legacy.

When he was finally discharged, he was taken on by the Lowestoft Theatre company in Suffolk, where he met the woman who would become his first wife, a green-eyed honey-blonde girl named Patricia Haines, who was the leading lady. They were married within a few weeks. She was the svelte daughter of a civil servant, he was a rough diamond with heavy-lidded seductive eyes and aspirations of grandeur. 'Michael was very attractive and charming and witty,' she would say later. 'But what really attracted me to him was his sense of humour and his professionalism.'

It was the pattern that scores of women would follow over the years to come. Caine himself would dismiss his appeal with one line: *"I'd always try to laugh them into bed . . ."* But there was no doubt about his approach or his appeal — they both worked.

That first marriage did not last, however. It broke down for one basic reason: the chemistry went sour. The couple found they were striking the wrong sparks off each other, and in the end they went their separate ways — Michael to live it up in London, Patsy to go home to her parents, and later remarry. 'Ours was a volatile marriage, doomed from the start,' she told friends. 'And not having any money made things worse.'

Caine was in the middle of his losing streak. Now he had lost a wife — although they had both gained a daughter, Dominique, born in 1956 when he was at a particularly low ebb, working in a steam laundry in Brixton. 'I was pushing trucks around the day she was born,' he recalls. 'All the other people there were black. I was the only white man who could stand the heat. They used to call me Sanders of the Steam Room!'

Patricia Haines died of cancer in Northampton in February 1977, when she was only forty-five. Caine attended the service in the tiny village church of Lois Weedon with his daughter at his side in the front pew. They had had their differences, but . . . 'It was my mother's death that finally brought Dad and me close again,' Niki said later.

Caine's own father died in 1956, the year of Dominique's birth, from cancer of the liver. Michael was shattered by the loss. Mr Micklewhite was fifty-six, and his weight had dropped from a burly fourteen stone to a scarecrow figure of little more than nine stone. It was a heart-rending sight, and Caine will never forget how he carried his father out of the house and into the ambulance to take him to St Giles Hospital. 'His last words to me were: *"Good luck to you, son"*. Oddly enough it was the only time he ever encouraged me, on his death bed.'

To recover, Caine went to Paris on his own. He needed time to reflect, time to consider his future. He stayed there six months, living rough, surviving the early weeks on £25 his mother gave him from her husband's life insurance, taking odd jobs and sweeping bars when he had to. 'It was my absolute all-time rock-bottom low,' he says.

When he came home he vowed he would never, ever, sink that low again.

His first act was to take on an agent: Ronnie Curtis, who ran a small battalion of hopeful actors from a first-floor office in Charing Cross Road. Michael would sit for hours every day on a wooden chair at the end of a row in the outer office, thumbing dog-eared magazines, drinking endless cups of tea, waiting for the blessed moment when the door to the inner sanctum opened and Ronnie would say: 'Right, *you* — want to be a policeman tomorrow?' Or an ambulance driver. Or a waiter. Or a soldier.

'We never stirred from that office. We were scared to leave in case we missed our big chance. It was the only way to get work. Strangely enough I always felt it was better sitting in that little room than working in rep . . .' Caine remembers. He felt closer to the mainstream of acting.

And slowly but surely the work started coming in. He played a sailor in *The Bulldog Breed*, and found himself threatening Norman Wisdom alongside a burly Teddy Boy named Oliver Reed. 'We were going to beat up Norman, which shouldn't have been too hard. We made nasty grunting sounds and growled: "I'm gonna bash your 'ead in" . . . it wasn't a very demanding part.'

But the film he looks on as his first real role was *A Hill in Korea*, about a small band of British soldiers enduring the hell of the Korean war and defending a vital hill. Another agent, Patricia Lathe, netted him that part, a lowly private with four lines to speak. A team of familiar faces had been recruited alongside him: sergeant Harry Andrews, lieutenant George Baker, corporal Stanley Baker, and fellow privates Michael Medwin, Ronald Lewis, Victor Maddern and Stephen Boyd. The film was made on location in Portugal. 'It wasn't really like Korea', said Caine, who had known it first-hand. 'The place that is most like Korea is Wales. But I didn't say anything. I liked the idea of going abroad, that's why.'

By now he had changed his name for the second and last time. The actors' union Equity had informed him that he could no longer be Michael Scott — they already had a Michael Scott as a member — if he wanted to pursue a professional career. For that matter they also had a Maurice Micklewhite already on the books. He vividly remembers that day in the West End of London when he came to terms with a new identity: 'All the names anyone could ever think of galloped through my mind. It's hard enough choosing a baby's name — and they're only Christian names. When you have to think up a whole new identity, it's frightening.' He tried to relax for a couple of hours by going to the pictures, and found his hero Humphrey Bogart was starring in one of his most brilliant portrayals —as Captain Queeg slowly going insane in *The Caine Mutiny*, which was in the middle of its run at the Odeon, Leicester Square. After the film Michael went across the square for a cup of tea, still agonising. 'Suddenly I looked up and there it was in great big red neon lights outside the Odeon: "THE CAINE MUTINY". I thought: that's it: It's strong and sharp. That's the name for me.'

He raced round to the Underground station, found an empty phone booth, called up Equity and demanded to know if there was a Michael Caine on the books. When the secretary said no, he told her: 'There is now. Book me in'. It cost him three guineas and he became Equity Member No. 6,922.

That new name seemed to open the floodgates.

Chapter 3
ZULU

In all, during the unsung years between 1956 and 1963, Michael Caine made no fewer than 125 appearances on TV and featured in thirty films, some of them with a few lines, others as merely an eager face in the crowd. He kept a meticulous record of each one, noting the role, the length of time he was on screen, the lines he had to say (if any) and a brief resumé of the plot.

That was before the film *Zulu* took him out of the shadows and into the spotlight. When the first notices came out for his role as Lieutenant Gonville Bromhead in that epic he threw the file away.

There were some lighter moments to ease the frustration. The first billing under his new name was a TV play on the story of Joan of Arc — performed live. The new Michael Caine marked the occasion by blotting his copy-book in style. He still comes out in a hot flush at the memory of it.

'I knew hundreds of thousands of people would be watching us. Everyone was on a knife-edge of tension. I was playing a guard, and I had to wear one of those helmets that looks like a 25 lb shell. My big scene was to enter a room at the top of a Norman tower where they were holding Joan of Arc, grab her by the arm and lead her out to be interrogated.

'For a start they were getting all the camera angles wrong. As I came in I knocked my helmet on the arch, and it went all lopsided on me. I was too nervous to do anything about it, and everyone told me later I looked like a slightly pissed guard.

In the first ten years of his acting career Caine made 125 TV appearances. Two of the most crucial were in plays by Johnny Speight: The Compartment, *with Frank Finlay, and* The Playmates.

'I had three lines, which I'd forgotten. When I turned round to take Joan out I found the camera had tracked in on me and was blocking the door. There was nothing else for it but to take the nearest exit—which unfortunately happened to be the window. So there's this unforgettable shot of me coming right up to the lens, staring into it in panic saying: *"Oh, bugger it!"* in close-up, before I hoisted Joan of Arc up on to the ledge and we both jumped out of the top of a Norman tower eighty feet up . . .'

He had a lot of TV roles like that — though without such disastrous consequences. Caine pounded the beat in *Dixon of Dock Green* as a copper, and went on the other side of the law in a later episode as a villain. Much of the time he played 'cheerful Cockneys', although it was a two-hander play by Johnny Speight called *The Compartment* which gave him his first real chance to prove himself as an actor. It was screened on BBC TV on August 22, 1961. Caine played a loquacious youth in a railway carriage trying to engage a stuffy businessman (Frank Finlay) in conversation — before producing a gun. He got good notices, and as a result was taken on by a new agent who has remained his friend and adviser ever since, Dennis Selinger of International Creative Management.

On the big screen the roles started to tumble his way, too. Small parts, true, but it was a living.

He played a German agent in the desert saga *Foxhole in Cairo*, and one of Hitler's aides in *The Two-Headed Spy*. To put the patriotic record straight he was cast as a cheerful Cockney sailor in *The Key*, a story of human relationships set against the war at sea, with William Holden and Sophia Loren. 'I spot a U-Boat coming up from below, go crazy with fear, fall overboard when a shell explodes near me, and I'm presumed drowned. But they cut the scene out of the picture — and I went with it.' Sophia? 'I never got to talk to her. She was the big star, and quite remote from the rest of us.'

Ending up on the cutting-room floor, a chastening experience for any actor, was something Michael learned to live with. He had no choice, anyway. Even more humiliating was the time he tried to play an Irish gangster in a B-movie called *Solo for Sparrow*, a thriller based on the Edgar Wallace novel *The Gunner*. On the first day at Merton Park studios the director, Gordon Flemyng, heard his attempt at an Irish accent and did not like it. Eventually, with Caine standing by, he consulted the script, produced a red pencil, sliced a few lines through it and announced: 'I think we can get away with it. We're going to have to make you deaf and dumb!'

Caine, still smarting from the insult, can afford a reminscent chuckle now. 'That's how we did it. I flapped my arms around and made mouthing signs, and the only way anyone realised I was Irish was when someone said: "Hey, Mooney, is that you?"'

He was learning the hard way. 'I spent the majority of my life being a loser and I know what it's like,' he'll tell you now. 'I think it must show in my acting: thirty years a loser, twenty years a winner. Thank God the losers are often more interesting than obvious winners.'

But he kept trying. And to gain experience he set foot in the West End theatre, as understudy to Peter O'Toole in the New Theatre production of *The Long and the Short and the Tall*, back in uniform as a British Tommy sweating it out behind enemy lines in Malaya. The cast included Robert Shaw, Edward Judd, Frank Finlay — and Harold Pinter. Caine stayed backstage for three months, restlessly watching O'Toole give a harshly realistic performance as Private Banforth, and wondering when he would get his chance.

'To be an understudy is the worst of all possible worlds. You're either bored witless, or you have to go out there and you're terrified, knowing that the audience has paid to see someone else,' he declares.

Finally O'Toole left: to star as Lawrence of Arabia in David Lean's masterpiece that would make him an international star. Caine took over for a seven-month tour of the provinces, with another young Cockney actor, Terence Stamp, earning his stripes too, taking over from Shaw. Michael was still unknown: still lagging way behind his contemporaries.

But when they got back to London, there was a message from his agent: a big-budget movie was pending and Caine was up for a role in it. The film was called *Zulu*.

Michael Caine sat alone in the rear of the chartered Comet, lost in thought. The more closely he studied the script, the greater came a surge of excitement and anticipation. This was his big chance. He knew it, and he was not going to throw it away.

The concept of *Zulu* was enormous. To do it justice the project would be filmed across a vast canvas in the Drakensberg Mountains in Natal, in the heart of Zululand itself, filled with stunning action against a background of awesome scenery. The story of the Battle of

The stance, the stiff upper lip, the mannerisms, were totally against his own character, but Caine's impact in Zulu was undeniable.

Rorke's Drift in 1879 was the kind of heroism that would stir the blood for decades to come, as the thin red line of British troops trapped in their compound heroically struggle to stem the tide of Zulu warriors threatening to overwhelm them.

Originally Caine had been in line for the role of Private Henry Hook, the con-man Cockney who was happier lying in his bunk bemoaning the conditions, the flies and the discomfort than helping his comrades outside — though when the chips were down he, too, was awarded one of the eleven VCs of the action. In the end James Booth got the role — and stayed in Britain for the interiors at Twickenham studios. The rest of the cast flew to South Africa for three gruelling months in the wilds.

Caine, to his total surprise, was given the part of Lieutenant Gonville Bromhead, on an intuitive whim of the director, Cy Endfield. Unlike other generals in the film field of battle, he had seen cinematic officer potential in the fair-haired young actor with the challenging, blue eyes who had auditioned for him in the Long Bar below the Prince of Wales Theatre on a Sunday morning in April 1963. The actor Stanley Baker, playing the hard-man Lt John Chard in command of the tiny garrison, was also co-producer. Both he and Endfield saw Bromhead as a chinless wonder, a product of the old school treating the dangers of a Zulu uprising like a Saturday afternoon foray on the playing fields.

Caine saw him as something else. 'I found an account of the Battle in a bookshop in Charing Cross Road,' he recalls. 'My man was actually five foot six, with a black beard! I persuaded Stan and Cy that he should be a strong character, rather than a weak one, because in the end Chard overpowers him — and there would be a much more interesting clash of personality.

'I told them: "the Hooray Henries are caricatures of what those men were really like. I just don't believe the Victorian officer was like that".'

Baker and Endfield listened closely, and finally agreed. 'You're right,' Baker told Michael. 'Play him as though he believes in himself.'

'*Hot day, hard work!*' With those words Michael Caine put himself on the map, and he would never have to look back again. They were uttered by Lieutenant Gonville Bromhead as he rode into view by a shallow river where a group of soldiers, sweating under the hot

29

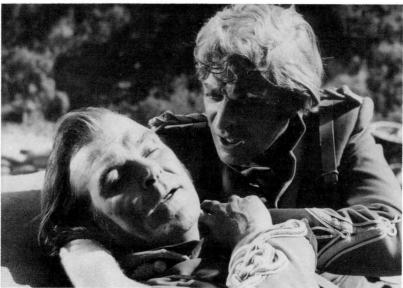

Stanley Baker was producer and star of Zulu. *He and director Cy Endfield listened carefully to Caine's proposals to give depth to his part.*

African sun, was busy building a bridge. Caine was resplendent in a red tunic, stiff gold collar and white pith helmet, with a sword at his belt and a pistol in a holster on his hip.

The first sentence, and the way he spoke it, established his character and his attitude in four words. The role, with its clipped upper-crust accent, was so far removed from the man himself that when people heard him speak in later films they questioned whether it was his real voice.

In sixteen weeks of filming, Caine had just fifty-two lines to speak, but he made the most of them. He was paid £4,000 and the film would take £12 million throughout the world.

When he was not facing the cameras or cooling off with a beer in the make-shift unit bar amid the kraal huts at the end of the day, Caine found he was examining the plumbing more than usual. 'I expect it was nerves, but I had the trots a lot of the time! I'd sit and stare at space through a hole in the lavatory door — that was my view of Africa! I even pushed out a knot in the wood so that I could see through it. To this day anywhere foreign causes me to head straight for the loo, and I blame it all on *Zulu*. Zu-loo!'

The film, and the performances of all concerned with it, still stands up today. The loneliness and isolation of the small band of men apprehensively waiting for a legendary enemy to appear on the horizon was unforgettably captured by the director of photography, Stephen Dade. Years later the 135-minute saga would be enlarged to an even bigger screen on Todd-AO to reflect its size.

The critics agreed. The *Evening News* headline was: I'D LIKE TO GIVE ZULU A V.C. OF ITS OWN, as the film critic, Felix Barker, declaimed: 'A triumph, filmed with rare coherence in the sense of period and the feeling of depth that it conveyed'. And in New York the *Times*'s Bosley Crowther first brought a new name to the attention of America when he wrote: 'Michael Caine is dandy as the second-in-command'.

And Caine himself? He was secretly delighted, but he kept his hopes to himself, merely nodding his thanks to the plaudits. Outwardly he stayed cautiously non-commital. With a thirty-year losing streak behind him, who could blame him?

Chapter 4
Harry Palmer... and Alfie

The praise was yet to be. First came one of those frustrating in-between periods, a creative menopause when Michael Caine could do nothing but play a waiting game.

In the four months while *Zulu* was being edited he spent most of his days and nights at the Pickwick Club in Great Newport Street, just around the corner from Leicester Square. Between 1964 and 1967 the Pickwick became the cornerstone of the swinging sixties, peopled by the luminaries who were hogging the headlines. It was a place for actors, artists, writers, designers, society photographers, models.

Caine was invited to join the Pickwick as 'one of the interesting and up-and-coming people'. He jumped at the chance. All right, he hadn't arrived yet, but something told him he was on his way at last. He liked the atmosphere, he liked the people, and he was aware that the Pickwick was the place to see and be seen in.

Among his cronies was Terence Stamp, the hot-eyed actor who was being hailed as Britain's new romantic hero after his big impact in Peter Ustinov's drama *Billy Budd*. The pair chummed up, and took a flat together in Ebury Street, where they swiftly made a name for themselves as two of the likely lads on the social register. John Barry was another contemporary, the composer of the thunderous music for *Zulu* and the creator of the cinema's best known spy score, the James Bond theme.

'We called them the Terrible Trio,' the club's founder and manager Desmond Cavanagh recalls. 'They were around all the time, even Saturday lunch-times when they would often be the only ones there. Mike was a leader of the social upheaval of the sixties, that superb explosion of articulate, intelligent working-class people. I wanted them around me.'

Leaning on the bar at his favourite corner position where he could study the passing throng, drinking lager at two shillings a throw because it was all he could afford, Caine saw them all: Noel Coward chatting with Princess Margaret, the Beatles in a hirsute mass, Marlene Dietrich, Sammy Davis junior, the gourmet Robert Carrier, director François Truffaut, Robert Graves, Kirk Douglas, Roger Moore, the Rolling Stones led by Mick Jagger . . . from royalty to the kings of rock'n roll, from millionaires to models seeking their own fortune, all of them flocked to the Pickwick.

The night when producer Harry Saltzman sat at his reserved table eating steak and pondering his new project was another rung of the ladder in Michael Caine's rise from obscurity to stardom. Saltzman was a tough, shrewd Canadian who had jumped on the Bond wagon and struck it rich with his partner Albert R. Broccoli by launching the incredibly successful super-spy James Bond into cinematic life. Now he was looking for something completely different — the antidote to Bond. The author Len Deighton had written a script which aroused his interest. It was called *The Ipcress File*.

'James Bond has spawned a lot of stupid copies of Superman secret agent heroes,' Saltzman recalls. 'Deighton had created a spy who was a loser. A real person. He looked like someone that bad things happen to. He doesn't get up and have champagne and caviare for breakfast, and he doesn't hop into bed with every beautiful woman that comes by. He worries about how to pay the rent at the end of the month.

'I wanted to project the anti-hero, someone people would identify with just as they fantasised with Bond.'

They had not even got a name for him, because the original character had been written in the first person. 'Our man was the sort of bastard who would do anything for a few pounds. He turned on his tormentors in the end, and took on the Establishment which had used him.'

Saltzman was having dinner when Caine arrived and took up his usual position on a corner stool in the bar. The producer eyed the tall actor in horn-rimmed spectacles with a thoughtful air. He had seen an advance screening of *Zulu*, but this young man didn't look or sound in the least way like officer material. 'He wasn't exactly scruffy, but he was certainly downbeat,' Saltzman recalls. 'He looked like an anti-hero and that's what I was looking for. An actor who would be believable.' He called Caine over, and invited him to sit down for a drink.

The result of that meeting was a seven-year contract, guaranteeing the actor a minimum £50,000 a year, and enabling Saltzman to take half of Caine's earnings on any film that he should make for someone else. 'The money was gigantic at the time,' Caine says now, adding: 'Though by comparison with what I earned later it became very small'.

First problem: the name. At a meeting in Wardour Street between Saltzman, Sidney J. Furie (the director) and executives from Paramount Pictures who were financing *The Ipcress File*, the discussion turned into an identity crisis. 'We've got to have a name for him,' Harry Saltzman declared. 'We can't go through the movie without one. We need something that means absolutely nothing, a common or garden name that means nothing at all.'

Out of the blue Caine piped up: 'Harry!' There was a long silence. Michael says now: 'It was terrible. I said it without thinking, and it was the biggest *faux pas* of all time. I was dreadfully embarrassed.'

Saltzman kept his face straight. 'Thanks very much,' he said. 'Just for that we'll *call* him Harry.' And they did. What's more, Harry Palmer wore spectacles, the first screen non-hero — or otherwise — to do so since Harold Lloyd.

'The glasses are a psychological advantage to me as an actor.' Caine has spent years analysing their appeal. 'When I take them off, people know there's going to be action.'

Harry Palmer's world was a seedy vision of uncarpeted rooms in bed-sit land, corruption and intrigue in high places. His file actually described him as 'insubordinate, insolent, with possible criminal tendencies'. His pay was £1300 a year, and he carried a Colt 32. How far could you get from the glamour world of James Bond?

The Ipcress File was undoubtedly the best of the three Harry Palmer films that were eventually made. With Furie's ability to cross-cut, backed by John Barry's chilling guitar score, the film achieved an extraordinary degree of palm-moistening tension, as Palmer gradually came to realise that one of his two superiors,

The Ipcress File — *Harry Palmer ('003½') the antidote to James Bond, moved in the shiftless, seedy world of real espionage.*

The torture scene in The Ipcress File.

intelligence chiefs Nigel Green and Guy Doleman, was a 'mole' working for the other side.

Deighton received £80,000 for each of his three stories, and was more than satisfied with Saltzman's choice. 'If I can't have Michael Caine I'd have Humphrey Bogart,' he declared. 'And he's dead.' One of the more publicised pictures that came out from the set was the day he educated Caine into *haute cuisine*, showing him how to break an egg with one hand to make an omelette.

With one accord the critics hailed a new star in a new role, confirming their earlier views on his performance in *Zulu*. *The Times* gave him a marvellous back-hander of a compliment: 'Whether the film will do for him what the James Bond films have done for Mr Sean Connery is doubtful — he is too good an actor for that.' Perhaps Judith Crist, writing for the New York *Herald Tribune*, encapsulated it best: 'You'll find yourself sweating out the ugly, plodding game of espionage along with Palmer in the heart of London,' she wrote. Meanwhile Michael Caine was making his own headlines on the social scale, and found himself in growing demand at parties, premières and charity functions. It was a surprisingly easy transition.

He expended half of the £4,000 fee from *Zulu* by moving into a plush three-storey flat over a hairdresser's salon at No. 5, Ebury Street, Belgravia, which he shared with Terence Stamp for two memorable years in which there was a constant stream of beautiful women parading in and out of his life. He enjoyed his new surroundings with quiet satisfaction. Each morning when he woke up in his large double bed on the top floor, surrounded by red velvet walls, with cushions scattered around the thick Oriental carpet, he would thank the lucky stars that had finally smiled down on him, remembering the other places in the mean streets of South London that had been his home.

Caine and Stamp had hit it off from the start, back on tour with *The Long and the Short and the Tall*. Together in Belgravia, they made a formidable team of bird-fanciers. Although Terry got the glamour girls — first Julie Christie moved in, then top model Jean Shrimpton took over — Caine was unobtrusively notching up his own score in the room upstairs.

Early on, Michael confided his technique with generous altruism. He told Terry: 'To seduce a woman, you've got to give her an excuse. Men and women like sex equally, right? But once the act itself is over

The author of The Ipcress File, *Len Deighton, teaches Caine how to crack an egg with one hand!*

37

and you're both lying in bed thinking about it, women need an excuse to justify it to themselves. So you have to give that justification.' Which is? 'Tell them you love them . . .' It was his technique, he used it unashamedly, and it worked like a charm.

He taught Terry the timing of what he called his 'hooded cobra' look. 'There's a moment when you're lighting a cigarette for a girl, and you give her the cobra look, straight into her eyes. It can be devastating when it's timed properly. They go weak at the knees!'

As Stamp confided later: 'Mike was like a guru to me. He taught me everything about the business, about living, about women . . .' Also: 'He would find humour in anything, and it was his wit and style that impressed everyone'.

Caine had learned fast, too. All the pent-up frustration that had lurked within him over the years was now being given free reign in a free-wheeling society where he was rapidly becoming an acknowledged leader.

While Caine enjoyed life and played the waiting game once more, he found himself hobnobbing with royalty in the shape of Prince Philip. Now one of the chosen set, Michael was celebrating his thirty-third birthday at Danny Kaye's rented flat in Chelsea, attending an informal party and chatting with the American entertainer in the kitchen when in walked the royal personage.

'Hullo,' exclaimed Philip. 'It's old Ipcress.'

'You saw it then?' Caine responded, taken aback by the introduction.

'Yes,' said Philip. 'We ran it at the Palace the other night. Funny thing, but I always feel I know people once I've seen them on the screen. Then when I meet them I find myself at a loss as to what to say to them.'

'If you'll pardon my saying it,' Caine rejoined, 'that is precisely the position in which I find myself at this moment.'

Suddenly it seemed as if the wheel of fortune was turning his way. *Zulu* was the springboard, *The Ipcress File* kept the coin spinning, and all he needed was confirmation that he was something more than a shooting star that had materialised in our midst.

One week later, *Alfie* came his way.

It took Caine one page of the script to decide: 'That's for me'. It began: *Alfie turns to the camera and says: Never mind about the titles* . . . Michael loved the whole approach. The character of the

Caine with Millicent Martin and Jane Asher in Alfie — *to this day he dislikes being identified with the womanising rogue that helped to make him a cult figure of the 1960s, and to gain him an Academy Award nomination.*

Shelley Winters' presence in Alfie *assisted the film in the US market.*

Cockney knave of hearts who took girls for the ride and discarded them like second-hand cars at the end of the affair was one he knew would appeal to women world-wide — however much they protested.

It was a brave gamble at a time when the age of the anti-hero was just being ushered in. The timing was perfect. Caine portrayed the role brilliantly, earned himself an Academy Award nomination — he was beaten by Paul Scofield for *A Man For All Seasons* — and managed to convey a brand new image with that hooded cobra gaze, the self-mocking approach and the marvellously deadpan throwaway lines.

Director Lewis Gilbert, who gave Michael another stab at an Oscar with *Educating Rita* almost twenty years later, assembled a full quota of females to be Alfie's playthings, only to prove how hell hath no fury like a woman horned: acerbic Millicent Martin led the field, followed by Jane Asher, Julia Foster, Eleanor Bron and even Shelley Winters, flown in from Hollywood to give the film an American lift.

It was scarcely needed. The film cost £350,000, and made £10 million in the US alone. Caine's profit? 'I got £75,000, and turned down a slice of the cake that would have made me three million dollars!'

In fact the film was held up for several weeks in America because Paramount Pictures, the studio that had backed *Zulu* and noted Caine's impact, were suddenly unsure of what a seasoned rogue like Alfie would do to the feminist market. In particular they were worried about his effect on powerful women's groups like the conservative Daughters of the Revolution, the Junior League, and lesser lights such as the Happiness of Womanhood society in Florida and the Radical Women Association in Seattle, all of whom would give tongue en masse at his ruthless quest for carnal delights.

Finally they took the plunge. And it paid off. American women decided they did like the blatant opportunist unleashed in their midst, queued around the block to see him in action, and bestowed the ultimate accolade in the memorable words of one Hollywood executive who publicly declared: 'Alfie makes Warren Beatty look like a novice!' The fact that the womanising image rubbed off in real life didn't worry Caine a bit. Now the social register included his name on both sides of the Atlantic.

Michael was developing his craft by leaps and bounds. Without specific stage-school training he had picked up useful tips along the

40

way. Like getting drunk. In one scene Alfie has to become legless, a mixture of laughter and guilt. Caine had worked out from an early age how to approach it.

'To be drunk you have to obey the principle that the man is trying to appear sober, that he's trying desperately to walk straight and speak properly. That is what drunks do.

'They don't try to fall all over the place — it just happens! A drunk is a man who is actually trying to stand up. When he goes down he does it very slowly, completely against his will. That's how I played it in Alfie, and since then in *Educating Rita*, *The Honorary Consul* and *Water*. The same principle still applies.'

By a gentle irony, it was Warren Beatty's sister Shirley MacLaine who, in the summer of 1966, called him person-to-person from California to invite him to fly to Hollywood — to be her leading man in a comedy-thriller called *Gambit*. Michael accepted on the spot. Secretly he had been waiting for the call – any call – to cross the vast no-man's-land of the Atlantic which to so many actors represents the gulf between obscurity and international fame.

In relative terms Britain commands a tiny percentage of the world's market in movie-going statistics: varying between four and eight per cent, depending on the year and the films. America meant something like 65 per cent, the quantum jump to real stardom.

At the same time, Michael missed his first Oscar. Being nominated as best actor for *Alfie* that April night in 1967 was an honour he had not really expected, and therefore he valued it all the more as it was an accolade from his peers and colleagues in the profession, the 4,000-strong members of the Academy of Motion Picture Arts and Sciences.

The fact that Oscar time is Hollywood's annual feast of self-indulgence, indigestible to many, a coast-to-coast live TV extravaganza with the whole razzmatazz of an industry paying its personal respects to itself . . . well, okay, that was part of the game.

To be fair, it was a 'strong' year. Caine was up against tough opposition. Richard Burton had been nomintated for one of his seven Oscar attempts, this one as the downtrodden schoolmaster in the vitriolic domestic slanging match with Elizabeth Taylor in *Who's Afraid of Virginia Woolf?* Alan Arkin was in the lists for the frantic comedy *The Russians Are Coming, The Russians Are Coming*, and Steve

McQueen was in for *The Sand Pebbles*. But the favourite was Scofield with his masterly performance as Thomas More in *A Man For All Seasons*, and privately Caine knew he only had a whisper of a chance.

When Bob Hope slit open the precious envelope and announced the foregone conclusion, Caine, applauding mightily in defeat, knew he was still a winner: 'Just being nominated means something rather special has happened'.

Twentieth Century-Fox were backing *Gambit*. Shirley MacLaine was cast as a shady Eurasian beauty involved in the theft of a priceless bust owned by Middle East financier Herbert Lom. The studio had been considering Sidney Furie as director, to keep the script fast-paced and moving. They had screened *The Ipcress File* for Shirley. It turned out that Furie was already committed, but MacLaine eyed the laid-back agent in the pale raincoat and said: 'I like the look of that guy in glasses. Let's have him as my leading man'.

'And that,' says Caine, looking back on the fickle finger of fate, 'is how I got my ticket to Hollywood.'

The launching party to punch that ticket took place in the exclusive Upstairs Room at Chasen's restaurant, with Shirley acting as official hostess. Caine stood around in the background, shuffling his feet, trying to appear at ease. It was not easy. 'There I was, first time out from England, and Shirley is standing beside me looking totally stunning to introduce this dummy from overseas to everyone.'

The first guest to walk through the door was Gloria Swanson, followed by Liza Minelli with Frank Sinatra as a close third. New lesson for Caine: 'Either you're accepted in Hollywood or you're not. That's the secret of the whole game. I was never so stunned in my whole life. Suddenly it was all there in front of me.'

But during that party came another lesson for the budding star: 'I really had a great time that night,' Caine recalls, 'except that right in the middle of it I was dancing away when I overheard someone say: "Who the hell is the guest of honour?" That brought me down to earth for a few minutes.'

The party was over, but the melody lingered on. It was faithfully reported in the two Los Angeles papers, the *Times* and the *Herald-Examiner*, filling column after column on the social pages with a batch of pictures to boot. Caine had arrived in style. 'Afterwards the phone never stopped ringing. I became a great social lion. I was invited everywhere — and I went everywhere if it sounded good.

'I was absolutely fascinated by Hollywood, but I was also very wary of it all. I'd been warned how the fame and glamour could go to your head, and that the big trip-wire was when you started believing your own publicity. My answer was to take it all with a sense of humour. I've tried to stay that way ever since.' And Shirley? 'She was my passport to glamour. She opened Hollywood to me. I'll never forget her for that.'

Meantime Michael set out to keep busy. He had already made a second film in England, an oddball comedy called *The Wrong Box* directed by Bryan Forbes with a macabre plot about two old men (John Mills and Ralph Richardson) trying to murder one another to inherit a vast fortune. It was peopled with an ill-assorted cast of character actors ranging from Tony Hancock as a bumbling detective to Peter Cook and Dudley Moore as a couple of avaricious nephews.

Caine's role was a naive, bespectacled medical student. He felt he needed a contrast to Alfie — 'I wanted to play a shy man with glasses. The trouble was, the film was what we call a scene-stealer: every time you walked on there was someone waiting to jump you!'

Whoever stole the scenes, the loser in the end was the box-office. The film died the death, despite black gems such as Caine's favourite scene where six hefty pall-bearers carry a tiny coffin containing the remains of a pet dog to the cemetery – instead of the planned cadaver – to be greeted by a shriek from the shocked widow: 'What 'ave they done to 'im? He was six feet tall . . .'

Chapter 5
Four-door-Ford

By now Caine's price had reached $200,000 a film. His star, as the astrologists might say, was in the ascendant. In fact, he was becoming a target for that kind of publicity; soothsayer Teri King prepared his chart and announced: 'Like all Pisces he is a complex character. Romantic yet cynical, sensitive, dramatic, restless, tending to expect too much'. And she located an 'ill-starred Jupiter' which tended to make Michael over-optimistic and also over-indulgent. She warned him sternly: 'The latter could very easily result in your becoming overweight if you are not careful'. How true. For the film *Death Trap* he had to shed twenty-five pounds in a month, and he has always had to watch his weight.

It was now, on his thirty-fourth birthday, that Michael Caine received another unexpected gift, one he had neither anticipated nor coveted: his seven-year contract with Harry Saltzman arrived by first post, neatly torn in half. 'I'll always remember opening that envelope and finding it. What a gesture! He wanted me to be free, and so he just sent it back.'

Saltzman, by now a millionaire several times over with the James Bond thrillers, says simply: 'We had become friends. I didn't need it'. He also knew that Caine would make any film for him if the script was right.

The script was right for *Funeral in Berlin*. Time to don Harry Palmer's spectacles again and shrug himself back into the white raincoat for the second Len Deighton spy tantaliser, this one directed with skill and precision by Guy Hamilton who had just finished

By the time of Funeral in Berlin *Caine's spectacles had become his trademark.*

Goldfinger, which to this day is rated by most critics among the best of the Bonds. Now he went from 007 to Harry Palmer, with a big budget and a story-line that brought 003½, as Palmer had been dubbed, into toe-to-toe confrontation with the KGB.

Caine reports: 'We filmed it in West Berlin, and I found the place fascinating. The atmosphere was unnerving. Every time we tried to film near the Wall the Russians used to bring lights and even mirrors out and shine them smack-bang into the cameras. When we finally filmed myself going across Checkpoint Charlie we had to do it with telescopic sights so that they wouldn't catch on.

'I thought it was a good picture. It was the first time anyone had shown on screen how two secret service outfits from Britain and Russia could work hand-in-glove to get information to please their masters.'

The critics disagreed. They found Deighton's cold-war complexities plodding and slow, and mourned its predecessor. *Ipcress File* had moved like a lightning flash. *Funeral in Berlin* simply lived up — or died down — to its title. Oddly enough, though, they treated Caine kindly, a benevolence that would track his footsteps all his career: however bad the movie, Caine somehow would always emerge comparatively unsinged.

As Ann Pacey summed it up in *The Sun*: 'Harry Palmer remains one of our more entertaining spies, and it is somehow comforting to know that there are crooks like him looking after us!'

Now came one of the surprise choices in Michael Caine's career: the steamy Deep South drama *Hurry Sundown*. The producer-director was Otto Preminger, the Austrian film-maker who once featured as the prison camp commandant in *Stalag 17* and, many held, had been playing the part ever since. Certainly Otto's megalomania around a film set was legendary. On every one of his films he took total command of the action from the initiation of a script through to the final snip and splice in the cutting room. The responsibility was his, and the bouquets and brickbats which came his way in mixed proportions were his alone to relish or endure. He would have it no other way.

In hindsight it was a mistake, but for Caine the role was a unique challenge. It gave him the chance to show the world a new accent, away from the monosyllabic deadpan voice he had assumed for Alfie and Harry Palmer. It also gave him the chance to spread his wings in

Oscar Homolka was Caine's friendly foe in Funeral in Berlin.

the hands of a director who, on a good day, could come up with a truly memorable picture and coax performances to match out of his actors.

On both counts, Caine blew it. The script described him as 'a virile young Southerner with an innate sense of bigotry and an acute lust for power'. It was a sweaty saga of racial tension and high emotion centred around land-grabbers in Georgia after World War II, as stubborn black farmers Robert Hooks and Beah Richards, supported by schoolteacher Diahann Carroll, fight to stave off the incursions of a modern canning plant. The script also handed Michael lines to say like 'Ah tho't yuh might be in need of a li'l restorative . . .' without cracking up, which he succeeded in surmounting — which is more than can be said for the critics when they heard it.

In fact it was Vivien Leigh, that one-time Southern belle from *Gone With the Wind*, who gave Michael a personal tip on the vocal nuances. Caine met her at a party in Hollywood shortly before he flew out to Baton Rouge in Louisiana to begin filming. He confided to her that he was having a struggle with the accent.

'There's only one way to beat it,' she told him firmly. 'Every time you're about to speak, say the words *Four-door-Ford* mentally to yourself.'

'I did, and it worked,' reflects Caine. And it did — up to a point.

Caine was disappointed, and admits it. 'People said I was miscast, but personally I think I took on more than I could chew. I just pushed myself too far. The truth was that I had been accepted as *Alfie*, and for years I couldn't live him down, whatever I did. It took *Sleuth* finally to bury him.

'The film was a very strange experience for me. We made it in Louisiana, and it was at a time when the black people were on the march through the south. We fell foul of the Ku Klux Klan, they even took a shot at our caravans as we were in a convoy on the way to one location. It was all very disturbing, and did nothing to help my concentration on the part.'

After that incident, when Preminger's distinctive white trailer was peppered with shotgun pellets from irate Klansmen hiding in the undergrowth, a 24-hour guard from the local sheriff's office was put on the entire unit. It was redneck country, and Caine was getting his first taste of racism.

'Everyone asks me if I was frightened of Otto, knowing his

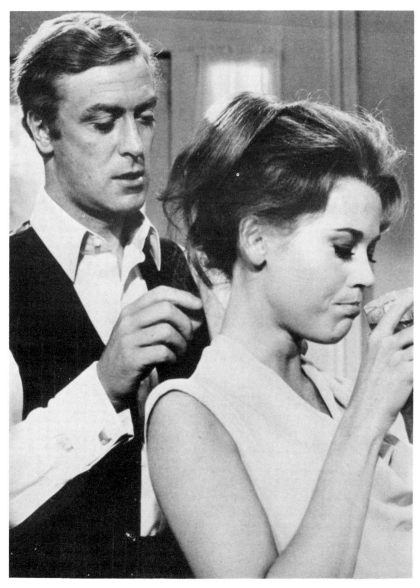

Hurry Sundown — *Caine's accent drew hoots of ribaldry from the critics. Jane Fonda, his co-star, he found 'feminine and vulnerable'.*

ferocious reputation. But we became instant friends. He had taken a shine to the Alfie character, and that helped break the ice. I was never scared of Otto. The Ku Klux Klan — yes, I was more frightened of *them!*'

Looking on the positive side, as he always tried to do, Caine came away with one useful piece of know-how: 'I learned the way to handle long takes. Otto loves them. Some of those shots went to seven minutes, and that's a *long* time on a movie. Even today, when I see them, I'm proud of them'.

After the stresses of the Deep South, it was time to climb back into the more familiar garb and accents of his favourite spy. Caine had taken a liking to Harry Palmer, even though the third adventure in the screen triology had to be the most outlandish of them all.

Billion Dollar Brain was the name of a computer colossus operated by power-mad Texan millionaire, Ed Begley. Our man is still hard up and hungry, but now he's running the H.P. Detective Agency. Harry is called back into service to outwit and defeat another master plan to conquer the world.

The director was that enduring *enfant terrible* of the British cinema, Ken Russell — 'a brilliant director and an emotional genius,' Michael sums up succinctly. '*Billion Dollar Brain* was a highly complex thriller, which needed a draughtsman. The last thing it wanted was an emotional genius. But the film was visually stunning'.

It was more fur-coat than raincoat weather as Caine found himself transported into the Arctic wilds of Finland, several degrees north of Helsinki, plodding through ice and snow and wishing he was somewhere warm and sunny. Finland proved not to be the happiest location for him. Physically it was not only arduous — on occasions it became positively dangerous, even for the star of the show who is supposed to be protected by stunt men and technical expertise.

'On one scene Ken had me leaping from ice floe to ice floe, which is a death-defying thing. My Finnish stand-in told me afterwards that if I'd fallen in they wouldn't have been able to get me out. Ken was using those telescopic lenses that he likes so much, and although they start out on you in long-shot when you could use a double you're into close-up at the end. You can't cheat.'

It was in this film, but back in the comfort of the studios at Pinewood, that Michael's younger brother Stanley was featured in a one-line role, playing a postman delivering an important parcel to

Two Caines — Michael and his younger brother Stanley during the filming of
Billion Dollar Brain.

Palmer. He would be back on screen again, as a small-time crook in *The Italian Job*, before deciding to quit and leave the stage to Michael.

Like the location, the film was something Caine would rather wipe off his personal file. Sadly, Harry Palmer's farewell was covered more in confusion than glory. The story was a hotch-potch of red herrings and bewildering confrontations, and quite who was doing what to whom was as clouded as the long Arctic night. Afterwards Caine said tersely: 'Ken Russell lost the story somewhere, and no-one cared a damn about what was going on because they couldn't follow what *was* going on!'

In his next film he repaid a debt to Shirley MacLaine, his Hollywood mentor, by strolling on for just three minutes in a silent cameo role in *Woman Times Seven*. Shirley herself appeared in seven episodes in a variety of vignettes, and all Caine had to do was amble along the Champs Elysées and end up sitting on a bench. It enabled her to put his name on the titles, which didn't hurt the box-office — even if the end-result was more becalmed than making waves. Caine didn't mind. 'I'd do anything for Shirley because she was so great to me in Hollywood,' he avers.

Those who know him well testify that this is true: Caine will never forget a favour — or an insult. People who, he feels, ignored or slighted him in the days when he was a nobody will find themselves up against a brick wall of implacability if they come fawning around hoping for a smile and a handshake of forgiveness. Behind the heavy-lidded blue eyes and the disarming spectacles lies a ridge of steel.

One who fell foul of Caine's less than forgiving nature was a film-maker named Peter Whitehead. At this point in Michael's career he found himself, to his total surprise, boosted as a star in a movie called *Tonite Let's All Make Love in London* 'produced, directed, photographed and scripted' by Peter Whitehead. It was designed as an arty documentary to capture the flavour of 'swinging London' with a host of star names led by Mick Jagger, Julie Christie, Lee Marvin, and Vanessa Redgrave, backed by music from the Pink Floyd.

The picture suddenly surfaced at the Academy. 'The cheek of it,' fumed Caine. 'Someone had come on the set of *Funeral in Berlin* and filmed an interview with me. Next thing I find I'm in this film. Of

52

course we slapped a solicitor's letter on them, and it was withdrawn.'

To cool off, Michael headed for the Mediterranean, and a curious suspense thriller called *Deadfall*, filmed in the south of France with a turgid script and direction (by Bryan Forbes) to match. Caine's role was a cat burglar with two accomplices (Giovanna Ralli and the authoritative Eric Portman) out to rob millionaire David Buck of a hoard of diamonds. There was a secondary plot involving incest, homosexuality, and lust which did nothing to add much interest to a film that emerged as less than average entertainment. It was another 'dog', as the Americans might say — and did — for Caine. But two unexpected scenes showed the film did have its merits: the discovery of the gems hidden as gleaming crystals in the chandeliers, turning the chateau into an Aladdin's cave of wonderment . . . and the jolting deadfall itself, with the thief dropping like a stone eighty feet from roof gutter to balcony to windowsill, with only his strong fingers preventing him from a sticky end on the cobbled courtyard below. Unfortunately these two scenes could not quite save the picture.

Chapter 6
'Hang on, I've got a great idea...'

Now came the toughest role Michael Caine had yet attempted. The film was *Play Dirty*, a war saga set in the Western Desert though actually filmed in Almeria, Spain — at that time fast making a name for itself as the home of 'spaghetti' Westerns. Caine's character was the uncompromising Captain Douglas, a man doing a dirty job and hating it, but determined to carry it through to the bitter end. Hollywood veteran André de Toth, once married to Veronica Lake and complete with piratical black eye-patch, directed the drama of a Long Range Desert Group of stubble-chinned irregulars (Nigel Davenport, Harry Andrews, Nigel Green, Daniel Pilon) on a mission behind enemy lines to blow up Rommel's petrol supply depot in the days leading up to El Alamein.

Caine recalls Almeria with the shudder of a man who has since had it written into his contract that he will never, ever, make another movie there. 'You'll find six sand dunes in Almeria,' he will tell you today, as bitchy as a guide from a rival resort. 'We would charge round a hill chasing Rommel's tanks — and find horse muck all over the desert and a stage coach hurtling off in the other direction pursued by a horde of Indians! We were forever wiping out hoof prints to get our war zone right.'

Adios, Almeria . . . hola, Majorca! As spring turned into summer, Caine jetted across that forty minutes of water to Palma, thence to a remote bay where Guy Green was struggling to make sense out of the complexities of John Fowles' eerie tale *The Magus* for the cinema and direct it.

It was a contract movie, one of several Michael had rashly signed to make for Twentieth Century-Fox following his Hollywood debut in *Gambit*. It meant he had to accept certain properties they put up for him while remaining free to go his own way on others. The Hollywood shark was showing its teeth, and Caine found himself wriggling uncomfortably in its grasp. 'I either had to do it, or I would be taken to court,' he growls now, still angry at the impotence of his situation.

He did not like the subject, and neither did he like his role as a schoolteacher — a man tormented by his dreams on a remote island set in the Aegean. What is more, he was not enamoured by the slavish attentions foisted on his co-star, Anthony Quinn. Quinn played the wealthy Conchis indulging his 'god game' to toy with lesser beings like the tutor (Caine) and the mystery woman (Candice Bergen) who wore an irritating smile and not much else of significance.

'I just couldn't stand the way Quinn's lackeys ran around doing his bidding,' Caine says flatly. 'My basic attitude to him was nothing special: I'm Joe Schmo and he's Morry Smith.' It wasn't the big fish so much as the eager minnows around him that Caine despised. He has never needed an entourage to bolster his own ego, and still finds it strange if other actors do.

But now at last came the movie for which not only Michael Caine but also his growing legion of faithful fans had been waiting for: *The Italian Job*. It was as fast-paced as its theme — an ingenious armoured-car robbery that involved stalling the computer that controls the traffic in Turin, pride of Italy's road network, and getting away with the gold in the middle of Europe's most stupendous traffic snarl-up.

The getaway vehicles were souped-up Minis, the robbers were a bunch of small-time British crooks, and the master-mind was Noel Coward as the urbane Mr Bridges, ruling his kingdom from a luxury prison cell like a Mafiosi chief. The plot was scarcely plausible, but for sheer entertainment value the picture came over as one of the best in that era, to be repeated on TV over and over again for light evening viewing. One of the most amusing touches was the moment when Caine, as the brash crooked Charlie Croker, broke into the prison loo to discuss terms with the *capo*, thus disturbing Mr Bridges' 'natural rhythm'. It was the only time in the script that they fell out. Caine's personal memory of the imposing Mr Coward:

Caine with Anthony Quinn in The Magus — *but he fell out with Quinns' entourage.*

Noel Coward's 'natural rhythm' is interrupted by Caine's breaking into jail in The Italian Job.

'I asked him about the drawbacks of living in Switzerland. *"Dear boy,"* he responded, *"The main problem is that it's so perpendicular!"'* One to be treasured.

The ending of that comedy-thriller still remains one of the prize cliff-hangers, literally, in screen history. The gold bullion is hauled into a coach and stored at one end. The driver, carried away with success, skids on a clifftop and the coach goes over the edge, hanging in space in perfect symmetry. The robbers are trapped at one end, the loot at the other. Stalemate? Not quite. The film's final line has Caine, deadpan as ever, delivering a laconic last thought: *'Hang on, I've got a great idea. . .'*

How to solve the insoluble? Audiences were debating it for months, and the ebullient director, Peter Collinson, revelled in their dilemma. There *was* no answer. Or was there? Caine and the script-writer, Troy Kennedy Martin, worked it out thus: 'The idea was that we'd leave it open. There was one way out, and it would make a great sequel — the coach is teetering on the brink, and we've got to get the weight from the back where the gold is stored, right? So near and yet so far.

'What we do is get them all to sit there sweating it our for five hours with the engine running to use up petrol from the tanks at the rear. Then the weight swings up. . . and everyone piles off as the gold goes over the cliff with the coach to start off another big chase. . .'

Caine's own chase after good roles led him back to World War Two, and a massive screen tribute to the RAF heroes of the Battle of Britain. Harry Saltzman and one-time Polish war hero Benjamin Fisz were the producers, and they brought in the accomplished Guy Hamilton to direct this £5 million epic of heroism and jingoism on the big scale. The cast list read like a battle-roll of screen honours: Laurence Olivier was Air Chief Marshall Sir Hugh Dowding, Chief of Fighter Command, with a supporting list of lesser ranks headed by Ralph Richardson, Trevor Howard, Kenneth More, Robert Shaw, Harry Andrews, Michael Redgrave, Nigel Patrick — and Michael Caine.

Michael was cast as Squadron Leader Canfield, a character made up of a number of real-life airmen, and in truth he felt he was too young for the role. He was swiftly put right. 'I was 36. But a real ace called Ginger Lacey, one of the advisers on the film, told me: "Actually, you're a bit old". In the war they were pilots at 19 and if

' 'Ang on- I've got a great idea!' Famous last words in The Italian Job. . . .

As Squadron Leader Canfield in The Battle of Britain.

58

they weren't squadron leaders by the time they were 24 there was something wrong with them.'

The end-result was a drum-banging tribute to British heroism, but with very little genuine character definition between the aerial dog-fights. Caine was proud to be part of it. If he hadn't been, he knew it would have been noticed as a sin of omission. His ultimate satisfaction was in the number of Battle of Britain pilots who personally wrote or telephoned their appreciation to Saltzman's office in Mayfair of a job well done.

Out of the blue at this flourishing moment in his career came a role that was tailor-made: Private 'Tosh' Hearne. He was a sharp Cockney sparrow of a soldier on the loose in World War Two with a bunch of his mates in the unlikely confines of a Pacific island with the Japanese lurking around every tree-trunk. Reluctant soldiers all, they preferred to laze in their jungle compound and let the war pass them by rather than risk an enemy bayonet.

No such chance in *Too Late the Hero*. Under the direction of Robert Aldrich, an amiable man whose geniality covered a formid-able record of over-violent films (e.g. *The Dirty Dozen*), their indolent life-style turned into a blood-bath for survival as they were summarily recruited into becoming a bunch of intrepid commandos on a death-or-glory mission to destroy a Japanese wireless station hidden in a remote jungle lair.

It carried its own brand of savagery, backed by nail-gnawing tension as audiences sweated alongside the blood and gutless troops on their thankless mission.

Once more Caine found himself recruited into the ranks with some familiar faces trudging alongside him: Captain Denholm Elliot, twitchy and remote, led the party. Lance Percival was promoted to corporal. Ian Bannen, Percy Herbert, Ronald Fraser and Michael Caine stayed as privates, bringing up the rear.

The point of the exercise was to take out a powerful Japanese transmitter monitoring the US fleet from the northern corner of the island, and then broadcast fake messages to the enemy before wiping out the base. US commander Henry Fonda orders the raid. Lieutenant Cliff Robertson goes along for the ride, to add extra appeal in the American ratings. Three of our boys are accidentally shot by their own men, the rest disintegrate into near-mutiny. Not

Reduced to the ranks in Too Late the Hero.

'One of the best performances I ever gave.' But the critics disagreed and the public stayed away from The Last Valley.

too good for morale, but the film becomes an intriguing battle of wits and eventual courage between Caine and Robertson.

Interestingly, Aldrich was pressured by the distributors to have two endings: one for the European and international markets, in which Caine would survive; the other for the US, where Robertson would come through. He refused. Cliff was given the actor's bonus of a gory death scene in the final reel — 'too late the hero'.

'It was a sweat,' Caine recalls. 'It isn't easy trying to remember your lines when you're stuck in the middle of the jungle in 120 degrees of heat, covered with flies and mosquitoes, attempting to give a performance at the same time. Physically it was the most difficult picture I ever made.'

He was hyper-sensitive of his work, insisting that 'unfortunately the film didn't work out'. But uncritical audiences found it gripping, even if one critic pointed out: 'Just see how quickly the lower-paid actors are picked off!' *The Times* also noted: 'Anyone rash enough to put on a British or Japanese uniform and stray within twenty yards of Mr Aldrich's cameras can enjoy a life expectancy of five minutes before being blown spectacularly into a thousand tiny pieces.' It was that kind of movie.

Caine inherited one unexpected bonus from the Philippines — a local beauty named Minda Feliciano, a lady he had met on a blind date in a Manila hotel. She was part of the high-society cocktail belt the daughter of a cabinet minister, petite and exotic, with haunting dark eyes and raven hair. She found him: 'Amusing, witty and quite devastating'. He took her home to England with him, and soon their names would fill many column inches in the gossip pages. Their affair lasted two years.

Michael Caine's price, like his star, was rising. For the first time he passed the half-million mark, in dollars. The film was *The Last Valley*, an under-rated historical drama set in 1641 in which he sported a red beard to play the leader of a bunch of lawless mercenaries in the Thirty Years War. Many observers still rate it his best performance, though it went unsung apart from the magazine *Films and Filming* which voted him Best Actor for 1970 in its annual survey.

It was shot amidst the picturesque scenery of the Austrian Alps, as Caine and his men stumble across a peaceful valley where the villagers live their tranquil life far removed from the ravages of war. After initial threats of death and mutilation to the locals, the red-bearded leader is finally persuaded by a refugee schoolmaster, Omar Sharif, to rest his men up for the winter, and try to forget a war that had lost its meaning for all of them.

The film was scripted, produced and directed by the multi-faceted James Clavell, author of massive novels like *King Rat* and *Shogun*. Caine became totally involved in the subject. He took enormous pains to infuse his character with qualities beyond even the script's demands, turning the outwardly ferocious commander into a man of ideals, fighting a war with himself as well as the enemy.

'To me this was the most disappointing picture I ever made,' Michael freely admits today. 'Not from the final product, but from the reaction to it. Personally I rate it one of the best performances I ever gave.

'It was the first time I tried a German accent, and I approached it the same way I would play a drunk: I played it like a German trying to speak perfect English.' He went as far as to buy dialect records and played them over for three days, listening intently, copying, rehearsing. And after all that? 'It meant nothing to the public, and the critics were extremely unkind.'

That they were. 'This is one of those big foreign-made epics where you spot familiar faces emerging from their chin stubble, but quickly lose the thread of who is fighting who, and why,' one summed up with callous disregard to the subtleties involved. Maybe he was right, because the public agreed on the verdict.

One intriguing side-light into Caine's new confidence came when his co-star drew him aside in a room in a Paris hotel where they had been holding an initial script conference. Sharif took his arm. 'How will we decide whose name goes on the credits first?' he asked. Caine frowned thoughtfully, as if it was the first time such a problem had occurred to him. Sharif paused a moment, then ventured: 'I think it should be the one who has the most money from this?'

Caine knew the normal rule in such cases when two major stars are above the title: the billing goes in alphabetical order. He nodded. 'Yeah, okay,' was all he said. A week later he ascertained Sharif's price: $600,000. He rang his agent, Dennis Selinger. 'Hold out for $750,000,' he ordered. He got his fee. And first billing.

Despite that, the general verdict was practically unanimous: thumbs down. So where to now?

The answer: back into strictly commercial pastures.

62

Chapter 7
Settling down

'It's a very, very violent film, even by today's standards.' Director Mike Hodges was giving his considered opinion on a picture that startled both the critics and the public who up to then had only suspected the chill layer of threat that lay behind Michael Caine's cold-eyed stare and carefully patterned monotone.

The film was *Get Carter*. It was based on a book called *Jack's Return Home* by Ted Lewis, and charted a backstreet saga of racketeering and mayhem as a big-time London villain comes north to discover the cause of his brother's sudden death.

Hodges was one of the cinema's new whizz-kids, a compact, ginger-bearded bundle of creative dynamite, emerging from the breeding ground of television into the challenge of big-screen drama. He could handle multi-million-dollar sci-fi epics like *Flash Gordon* with the same ease with which he made his initial mark in a 90-minute gangster drama for TV called *Rumour*, which was basically a run-up to *Get Carter*.

Caine had no illusions about his role. No soft-pedalling, no compromise. He put his neck on the line, going all out to reflect the shocking violence that exists in the criminal element behind the facade of urban city life. He blasts his foes with a shotgun, uses a knife on one victim, throws another over a penthouse balcony, and even plunges a hypodermic syringe into a local hooker to shut her up, leaving her floating naked and dead in a pond.

Hodges declaimed with some pride afterwards: 'The real villains come out from the cinema and say it's one of the best pictures they've ever seen. They're proud to be portrayed accurately instead of looking like idiots'.

Caine puts it another way: 'We made it deliberately violent, because I'd seen so much rubbish on TV. People keep getting hit in the face, and you have fights in Westerns where there's never any blood. . . No-one ever seems to get hurt. That to me is a far more dangerous violence. Young children watch it all the time, and they think that if they hit someone in the face nothing happens. . . This film shows it differently. We showed you that it *hurts*. I happen to think that it's a brilliant film, with a brilliant director.'

The film cost $750,000, which coincided with Caine's going rate. But he had become part of the 3M Company — Mike Hodges, director: Michael Klinger, producer; Michael Caine, star. . . so he took a large slice of the cake instead. And it was a crucial role for him: 'As far as I was concerned, up until that time I'd always been playing nice people. Even Alfie was nice in his way. This one was an absolute and utter brute, which was my way of satisfying myself and perhaps showing the public a thing or two besides. . .'

The critics responded by using terms like 'revolting', 'bestial', and 'gratuitously sadistic', all of which encouraged the great mass of the public to crowd into cinemas up and down the country to witness the apparent orgy. Caine's own final word was: 'You can despise Carter. But that kind of man usually only hurts his own kind. It is controlled mayhem.'

Back on top of the world, Michael Caine pulled the plug neatly on himself by taking on a role that in hindsight looks like an act of sheer lunacy. *Kidnapped* remains his personal nightmare to this day both in terms of non-enjoyment while making it, lack of funds to deem it worth the effort, and audience reception.

Caine played Bonnie Prince Charlie's loyal aide Alan Breck, sported a sandy moustache, buckled a swash or two and did his best to make Robert Louis Stevenson's character emerge as a Scarlet Pimpernel, when he knew that in reality 'Alan Breck was a drunken, murdering soldier of fortune'.

More important from a practical point of view, Caine found his finances less than satisfactory from the experience. Still bristling, he declares: 'It was a disaster from beginning to end'. Sometimes there's no business like no business.

It was at this point in his life that he came to terms with his future.

After years of strident bachelorhood, footloose and fancy-free for so long, Michael Caine was starting to feel the need for a more stable life-style. 'I realised one day that I wanted a comfortable home of my own, not just a pad. And I wanted someone to share it with.'

His pad up to now had been a five-bedroom apartment on the seventh floor of a luxury block at No 47, Grosvenor Square, opposite the American Embassy. There were four bathrooms panelled in pink marble, and the taps were gold. It was spacious and elegant, and a major step up the scale from the house he had shared with Terence Stamp before they went their separate ways.

But now he hungered for something more, a place where he could set down roots, and fulfil a dream he had secretly nursed since those days when he was evacuated as a wide-eyed city boy to rural Norfolk. He wanted space and the sounds of a flowing river. And in the two-centuries-old Mill House in Clewer Village near Windsor Castle, he found both. The Thames was close by, and a mill stream ran below part of the building and on through the seven aces of fertile land as part of the irrigation, which was further increased by a trout stream.

Caine purchased the estate for £50,000 when it was run-down and over-grown, and over the ensuing months redesigned it to his personal requirements: every room had its own decor and furniture, from traditional English to opulent Oriental, and the guests who sampled them included Roger Moore, Robert Bolt, Peter Sellers, and Harry Saltzman. If they weren't on the tennis court or lounging beside the swimming pool, there was a games room stacked with pinball machines to while away the leisure hours. For Caine, it was his Shangri-la — 'a magic place'.

As a complete contrast to the frenetic disco life in clubs like trendy Tramp's or ritzy Annabel's, Caine could now be found spending hours at a time in the extensive vegetable gardens, even driving a tractor to plough some of the acres. 'Gardening is the best therapy I know,' he declared. 'Actors in the States spend thousands of dollars on a psychiatrist — at least I know that if I spend it on my garden I'll never have to stretch out on a couch!'

Instead he found himself stretching out in bed with two women — Elizabeth Taylor and Susannah York — in a marital drama called *Zee and Co.*, directed by Brian Hutton from an original screenplay by Edna O'Brien. Caine played an architect married to Miss Taylor, with a dress designer mistress (Susannah York) on the side. It was a glossy exercise in infidelity, with Liz Taylor going happily over the top as the volatile, insecure wife who finally realises her rival's weakness — and takes *her* to bed, leaving Caine gasping like a stranded fish on the sidelines.

Behind the scenes, there were problems. Edna O'Brien claimed that her script had been taken apart by the director, and bore little resemblance to the way she intended it.

Caine himself remains unsure of the backstage fireworks, even now. 'It was a strange film. All I know is that Edna O'Brien washed her hands of it altogether. I don't know why. It wasn't bad. It made money.' With his customary candour he adds: 'I suppose it was Liz Taylor's name. But she and I became great friends instantly, because she's a no-nonsense lady and I like to think I'm a no-nonsense man.'

It was the first time Michael had worked closely, even intimately, with a known superstar, and it gave him a chance to come to terms with his approach to them, to himself, to acting. 'I don't really give a damn about people's reputations. If you do, you're lost. Luckily Elizabeth was smashing to work with, a real knock-out bird. She doesn't come on strong at all.' Just as well. 'We'd hardly had time to say hullo when I had to start chucking her about on the bed. . .'

As with that earlier experience on *The Magus*, it was the superstar camp-following that roused Caine's ire: 'When you work with Elizabeth the people around her make it seem as if you're working with the Statue of Liberty!'

Now came *Pulp*, a comedy-thriller set in Malta and centred around an Englishman (Caine) living in the Mediterranean and making a living by churning out cheap penny-dreadfuls. He is approached by gravel-voiced Lionel Stander as a PR man ostensibly hiring him to ghost the biography of a retired Hollywood movie star (played by Mickey Rooney) whose speciality was gangster roles. Caine pounded his typewriter in his lonely room in a villa overlooking the sea, and produced the Mickey Spillane-type voice-over as well — 'a voice that reflected the man, tired and world-weary, but not a cynic,' as the director, Mike Hodges, put it.

It was one of those locations that should have been fun, but wasn't. Michael Caine took an instant dislike to Malta the moment he set foot on the tarmac of Valetta Airport, and the impression grew rather than receded over the weeks that followed. Why? Many reasons. He did not like the look of the island, finding it far too arid. He did not much care for the inhabitants, finding them in general deadly dull, and he was not over-happy about the way the film was turning out. 'I adore trees and greenery and gardens, and Malta is the only island I've been to that has no trees. It drove me bananas.'

As for the film: 'It's one of those things where you try to please everybody and wind up pleasing nobody'. In fact the picture ended up as an arty hotch-potch of ideas and comedy situations that led nowhere and left audiences feeling cheated of any real meat in either the dialogue or the action.

Towards the end of production, with nine weeks and a heap of boredom under his belt, Michael was asked by a radio interviewer for the BBC's World Service: 'Tell me Mr Caine, if there's one thing the tourist shouldn't miss in Malta, what is it?'

Caine's answer came back in a flash: '*The plane home!*'

It was at this point that Shakira Baksh entered Caine's life, and changed it radically. She had been Miss Guyana of 1967 in that annual parade known as the Miss World contest, and came third. As a result she earned herself a few walk-ons in low-budget British films like the *Carry On Again Doctor* comedy, where she played a native beauty on the exotic tropical island of 'Pizunwind'.

Michael spotted her on a coffee commercial for Maxwell House, and flipped on the spot. 'There was this lovely girl, and I knew I just had to meet her. I decided I would fly to South America and find her. . .' Instead he found himself at Tramp's disco-club that night chatting to a fellow actor and raving about the unknown love goddess. 'Oh, she's in London,' said the other casually. 'D'you want her phone number?' Michael, hardly believing his luck, called her up, mentioned his name, and invited her out to dinner.

'She had just seen *Get Carter*, so I had a certain image to play down, first time out.' But the chemistry was there, and still is. Shakira was fourteen years younger, a tall slender beauty with a silken-smooth black skin and lustrous dark eyes. Back home she had been a librarian, then a fashion model. But it was her temperament as well as her looks that made a lasting impression upon Caine. 'She was quiet without being dumb. Shakira is incapable of quarrelling — she just doesn't answer!' Perhaps it derived from her Indian background? 'Yes, 'says Michael laconically, 'Indians are very quiet.'

On the obvious question of colour, Caine doesn't mince his words. 'The colour difference between us never presented any problem. I

Caine's vengeful gangland boss in Get Carter *startled his public because it was so violent. 'We showed you that violence hurts,' he explained.*

Two actors, two roles, two Oscar nominations — Laurence Olivier and Michael Caine in Sleuth.

never got any nasty letters — not a dicky-bird. You see, I didn't marry an Indian woman — I married a woman who turned out to be an Indian.

'Racially I feel what I say. I've never been a hypocrite. I'm quite prepared to offend anybody! My view is straight down the centre: politically I'm an extreme moderate and a complete liberal. I believe that some people hate other people because they're black, but I've also had people hate me because of my Cockney accent.

'The world is far too developed now for there to be any stigma with Shakira and myself, though thirty years ago it might have been different.

'People are afraid of being taken over, of losing our national identity. For myself, I don't see any colours or religions.' End of sermon. The complete liberal has said his piece, and means every word of it.

So Shakira moved into the Old Mill House by the stream, and lived contentedly with Caine for sixteen months before she discovered she was pregnant. Someone used those three little words: *Living in sin* — and Caine hit back with a ready retort. 'Sin is an opinion — and you cannot live in an opinion. Our options are clear and open, they always have been. Every step of the way Shakira and I knew what we were doing.'

He married her. The old-fashioned values drummed into him by his father dictated that there should be no stigma of any kind, real or imagined, that would be attached to his off-spring. And by now Michael was secure enough to know that he would never subject his second wife to the tensions and hardships accumulated in his first rash mariage. 'It wouldn't be fair on Shakira to land her with an actor who was going down,' he reasoned. 'I'm happy to share success. With failure, I don't want any witnesses.'

He proposed to her on Christmas Day 1972, following the family lunch at the Mill House with eighteen assorted relatives, including his mother Ellen, as sprightly as they come, and brother Stanley, along with a smattering of uncles and aunts and nephews and nieces in attendance.

After the turkey had been demolished, Michael spent an hour by himself walking around the grounds of his estate. Then he appeared in the doorway, beckoned to Shakira, and quietly told her: 'I have an idea. I think we should get married'. Shakira looked at him, nodded, smiled, and replied: 'That's a good idea — let's!' One month later they did, in Las Vegas.

Looking back, Caine will tell you now: 'I see my emotional life as a three-act play. The first act was my unhappy marriage. In between made all the headlines. This last act is the one that will linger.'

Now came an act of a different sort that was to linger as the most demanding and intricate of Michael Caine's entire career. *Sleuth* was a cat-and-mouse game of wits and suspense that had rightly earned its deviser, Anthony Shaffer, a unique reputation in the theatre. Just two players — executioner and victim, but which is which? — keeping the tension as taut as a violin string, and playing havoc with our minds and our nerves as we seek to follow the dead-ends and red herrings that abound. Everyone else, the police officers, the wife, were purely incidental.

The plot centres around Andrew Wyke, noted writer of detective fiction, who invites his young neighbour Milo Tindle to his rambling home in the country for an evening of conversation and free-flowing liquor.

Early on, the author reveals he knows that his guest is having an affair with his wife. But far from objecting — or so it seems — he has evolved a plan which will bring them both a handsome profit. A fake burglary, with Milo making off with the wife's jewels so that he can support her in style, and Wyke collecting the insurance money. The game is on.

When the casting was announced, it made the film world sit up in astonishment. Sir Laurence Olivier would play Wyke. And . . . Michael Caine would be Milo.

Caine accepted with alacrity. 'I thought: "With Olivier, I can't lose. If I'm not as good as he is, nobody will be surprised. If I give him a run for his money people will say: Fancy Michael Caine doing *that!*"'

In fact he was Olivier's choice, or one of them. 'He accepted the role of Wyke, and was asked who he wanted to play opposite him. He made out a list and gave it to Joe Mankiewicz (the director, whose previous work includes *All About Eve, Guys and Dolls, Suddenly Last Summer* and the ill-fated *Cleopatra*).

'Among them were Alan Bates and Albert Finney. Available made it me. I'd never met him, and my main worry was that he was Lord

Olivier. He's the only actor ever to be made a lord, and I thought: what do I call him?

'A week before we were to start, a letter came from him. It said: "Dear Michael, so happy we're working together. One minute after we meet, I shall call you Michael and you will call me Larry, and that's how it will remain forever".

'When we met, he said: "*Good morning, Michael*". I said: "*Good morning, Larry*". He said: "*Right, what page?*" And we went on from there.

'People thought I should be over-awed — but why? I don't think it's an actor's job to be over-awed. And to be honest I can't say I learned anything from him. But I'm willing to take on anybody on screen, and Larry paid me the greatest compliment by his attitude on *Sleuth* because he treated me in his performance as though I was as good an actor as he is. He never let up on me, never gave me an inch.'

It paid off, in prestige if not in box-office millions. The critics rose to them in unison. Felix Barker in the *London Evening News*: 'The verbal juggling of Shaffer's witty dialogue and the war to the death by the two stars make this the most fascinating screen battle for years'. And Ian Christie in the *Daily Express*: 'Superlative performances, an undiluted pleasure to watch'.

The final accolade came when both Olivier and Caine were nominated for the Best Actor award when the Oscars came up the following April. Against them were Peter O'Toole (*The Ruling Class*), Paul Winfield (*Sounder*) and the most popular runner — Marlon Brando for his relatively short-lived but memorable portrayal of 'The Godfather'. The film had become one of the most successful of all time, which counts for a lot among Hollywood's voters.

Brando won, and failed to show up. Instead he sent an 'Indian princess' emissary, which brought uproar to the Los Angeles Music Centre. Caine was livid. Not because he had lost, but at the manners of the winner.

'He should have been there. Doesn't he owe this town *anything*? He should treat the Oscar with the respect it deserves. Christ, if I had one I know I would. . .'

Chapter 8
Farewell, England

After the creative excitement of *Sleuth* and its aftermath of bouquets and the promise of great things ahead, a curious lull spread across Caine's career in the quality of scripts that came his way. He was busier than ever, but the films never quite came up to expectations.

He made *The Black Windmill* for Don Siegel, a noted American thriller specialist (*Riot in Cell Block 11, The Killers, Dirty Harry*). It was a story of industrial espionage that got lost somewhere between London and Paris, in the Sussex countryside where the black windmill of the title was located. Caine starred as Major John Tarrant, forced to raid his own Foreign Office safe of a cache of diamonds when an army syndicate kidnaps his son. Janet Suzman was his distraught wife, Donald Pleasence a paranoid MI6 chief. Despite such quality players, Caine felt he had to agree with the critics who dismissed it as 'a rather mundane thriller with little of the familiar Siegel crispness and tension'.

He moved on to *The Marseilles Contract*, more thrills with Caine as a lone assassin hired unofficially by the French police to kill a Marseilles drugs dealer (James Mason) with a laconic US agent (Anthony Quinn) as back-up. Caine died on his feet, shot dead in a gun battle. So did the film.

Now came another strenuous chase thriller, *The Wilby Conspiracy*, directed with his customary efficiency by Ralph Nelson and filmed in Kenya. The setting was South Africa, and a straightforward enough theme was complicated by a heavy-handed anti-apartheid message that merged somewhat uneasily with the action. Sidney Poitier was

The Wilby Conspiracy (*1975*).

The Romantic Englishwoman, *directed by Joseph Losey. 'I happen to agree that English women are romantic,' Michael Caine, cast against type himself, said. Glenda Jackson, his co-star, did not deny it.*

on the run with Caine — shades of *The Defiant Ones* — and their hunter was Nicol Williamson, chillingly effective as the bullish security chief stalking the two fugitives while enmeshing them in his own secret web of political intrigue.

It was on this film that Caine had a hairsbreadth escape from being killed — for real. The climactic chase through the bush took place on a rutted track near Lake Naivasha, with Poitier at the wheel of a stolen Jeep. Recalls Caine: 'Sidney was driving at 50 mph. They'd fixed a big Arriflex camera on the bonnet to film us against the background speeding by. Suddenly a bolt jarred loose, and the whole camera came unstuck and hurtled straight between the two of us at about 90 mph! Luckily there was no windscreen, so there was no flying glass. Just a camera exploding between us. There were bits of it everywhere, a £35,000 Arri written off! We were both of us shaking for a long time afterwards. We could easily have been killed.'

Back to quieter pastures, though challenging in a different way, was *The Romantic Englishwoman,* set in affluent stockbroker country with all its attendant cocktail parties and sophisticated after-dinner conversations. Caine was cast completely against his own character as a best-selling novelist whose wife (Glenda Jackson) leaves him without warning or explanation for the delights of Baden-Baden in midwinter, thereby fulfilling a long-cherished romantic vision.

The director was Joseph Losey, and with the formidable Miss Jackson at the height of her career as the most sought-after British actress of her decade, the film was quality material all the way. Caine was as fascinated by the concept as he was repelled by the characters. For him they represented total anathema.

'It attracted me because for the first time in my life I found myself playing someone that if I met in real life I would not only dislike but even despise! I don't like those sort of men who let it all go on around them without doing anything. It's completely against nature. At the minimum I'm a catalyst. But in the end I thoroughly enjoyed playing it because I submerged my own personality entirely and invented everything as I went along.'

And, never forgetting his public, he could not help adding: 'I happen to agree that English women *are* romantic, just as the film suggests. French women have a reputation for being romantic, but they're not. They're just practical. English women are the most romantic in the world.'

Predictably, he found Glenda Jackson 'a complete and utter professional. She is the best film actress I ever worked with. She is so aware of the difference between stage and film acting'.

Glenda Jackson herself counters generously: 'I don't think anyone realises yet just how good an actor Michael is. Also, he's amazingly honest, and that's very rare, especially in a profession when sometimes it's difficult to know what's real and what is fantasy. I like the delight he takes in what he has achieved.'

One fresh delight in Caine's life was his daughter, Natasha Halima, born July 15, 1973. Michael had been present at the birth, holding Shakira's hand at the bedside throughout the labour and delivery. 'A beautiful little girl,' was his verdict. 'But she has my eyelids, which make her look kind of sleepy.'

He made a brief return to Hollywood to star in *Peeper* (entitled *Fat Chance* in the US) playing a down-at-heel English private eye operating in LA in the late 1940s, and up to his neck in a hunt for a lost orphan girl. Natalie Wood played the obligatory nymphomaniac wandering through a plush mansion in revealing white silk, but the plot was soggy, and the film, like the subject, vanished almost without trace. Caine turned tail and headed back to Europe, fast.

And on to North Africa. *The Man Who Would be King* was a project in the big league, a Kipling adventure written in 1888, and set in the India of the times. It was a story that had haunted the veteran director John Huston for a quarter of a century. Originally he had planned to cast Humphrey Bogart and Clark Gable as the pair of seasoned rogues Peachy and Danny, whose adventures are chronicled amid the Himalayas.

But now it fell to Caine to take on the role of Peachy, once assigned to his childhood hero Bogart, with Sean Connery as his compatriot. The duo are former British army sergeants earning a dubious living by gun-running and smuggling, who invite Rudyard Kipling himself (played by Christopher Plummer) to witness a 'contrak' they have drawn up pledging them to set themselves up as kings in the Himalayan foothills and make their fortunes. Which is precisely what they do, encountering all sorts of hazards on the way.

The film was shot over fourteen long, hot, weary weeks around Marrakesh, where the hills and desert scrub was sufficient to pass muster as India with the average film-goer. Like Almeria, that part of North Africa has doubled for locations as varied as Mexico, South

Shakira Caine, Michael's wife, had one line in The Man Who would be King. *The filming of Kipling's story was the fulfilment of an ambition for John Huston, the director. Sean Connery co-starred with Caine.*

A grizzled chin and a German accent for The Eagle has landed.

Africa, India, Russia — and occasionally been allowed to pass as Marrakesh itself.

Caine spent two hours daily in the make-up trailer being transformed into a seedy beggar escorting a mad priest (Connery's disguise) through the north-west frontier. It was tough going — but rewarding. Caine had a role he liked, and he was working with a director whose own life had spanned decades, who had met them all, knew them all, could tell stories about Hollywood legends far into the night. As for the part itself: 'I loved it. It had so much going for it, however, depth of character, action, adeventure.

'There was no jealousy, no rivalry between Sean and me to steal shots. Nothing like that. Everyone *gave* all the time. It is the best relationship I ever had with an actor. If I'd been going to be overawed by anybody, it would have been Huston — but I had an ability to make him laugh. After three days he was calling us Peachy and Danny, and I realised he was watching his dream come true.'

Shakira Caine found herself with the last part she would take on in films, before being Mrs Michael Caine became a full-time role. At the last minute she was called in to replace Tessa (daughter of author Roald Dahl) as a tribal princess who married Danny when he was declared a god by the superstitious villagers. There were murmurs of nepotism, but in fact the choice was made by Huston himself, who decided the princess should be dark-skinned, not white. 'They told me someone else would get it anyway,' says Shakira. 'I was hesitant at first, but in the end I did it.'

She had only one word to utter in the film: 'Yes'. But the spectacular wedding scenes surrounding her were extremely arduous. Shakira was borne into a huge courtyard with 2,000 extras bowing and scraping alongside her. As one wit remarked, if she had got her line wrong and said: 'No', it would have changed the course of the movie and cost thousands. Shakira herself declared: 'It's the last time, I'm not anxious to be a star, anyway'. So — only one star in the Caine household.

The film came out, and *The Times* remarked on 'the lovely double-act of Caine and Connery, clowning to their doom'. Huston paid his own compliment: 'Michael is one of the most intelligent men among the artists I've known'. He would use him again, on *Escape to Victory*.

This was the busiest time of his entire career for Michael Caine.

Rapidly he moved on to *The Silver Bears,* which took him on another whirl around Europe masterminding a plan to swindle a Swiss bank of its assets. Then he was back in German uniform, complete with accent, in the wartime thriller *The Eagle Has Landed,* based on Jack Higgins' gripping best-seller about an audacious Nazi plan to kidnap Winston Churchill and spirit him back to the Fatherland.

Caine's role as Kurt Steiner, in charge of a band of crack German paratroopers dropped over Norfolk for their 'mission impossible' was a hard one. Not just because of the accent or the physical demands of the script, but the character himself. 'He's the heavy, but he's also a sympathetic German officer, the equivalent of the English Guards. They absolutely hated the Gestapo and the Nazis who were all bourgeois opportunists, simply yobboes! It went on for sixteen weeks, and it's very difficult to sustain something like that. For the voice I invented a very sharp clipped tone. There's none of that *Ve haf vays of making you talk!*'

The director was another Hollywood legend, John Sturges (*Gunfight at the O.K. Corral, The Magnificent Seven, The Great Escape*). 'Working with Sturges was marvellous,' Caine says. 'He is inclined to think: *Take One,* which I like. He doesn't care for Take Two at all'!

Next came a change of uniform for *A Bridge Too Far,* the massive war epic funded mostly with Dutch money that did for the people of Holland what *The Battle of Britain* did for the RAF. Sir Richard Attenborough was the director, shifting his men around like chesspieces. It was a fine memento to Holland and the battle of Arnhem, with Caine joining a host of celebrities in cameo roles, alongside names like Robert Redford, Sean Connery, Laurence Olivier, Dirk Bogarde, James Caan, a *Who's Who* with familiar faces popping briefly out of the smoke, mud and gunfire to speak their piece and head for the bank in a hurry!

At this point Caine took a career gamble by agreeing to appear in a couple of 'disaster movies', hosted by the indefatigable Irwin Allen, a Hollywood impresario who had made $100 million from *The Poseidon Adventure* and *The Towering Inferno.* His formula success was simplicity itself: 'Put a lot of people in jeopardy. See who makes it out and who doesn't'. It was a useful bonus if the people were rich and famous.

Caine was intrigued. After all, every other star in the business

The Swarm. *But the public didn't, despite an all-star cast including Caine, Katharine Ross and Henry Fonda.*

seemed to be doing them, and he wasn't going to be left out. So when Allen told him about a $15 million spectacular he was lining up called *The Swarm*, Caine thought to himself: why not? His fee was now into the million-dollar-a-movie bracket; and in concept the film was quite extraordinary.

Michael was cast as one Brad Cane, a macho name for a macho guy, called in when a swarm of giant killer bees from South America threatens to engulf the United States and sting the populace to death. A roll call of box-office names from Richard Chamberlain to Richard Widmark was brought in, including Henry Fonda, Olivia de Havilland, Katharine Ross and José Ferrer.

How was Michael to know — how was anyone to know — the film would become a laughing stock in Hollywood, and stretch across the Atlantic as a by-word for bad movie-making? If it wasn't the worst film he ever made, it was certainly the most expensive bad film. It was one of those films that is so bad that it becomes enjoyable, and generally the reception was a comic raspberry.

Caine valiantly admits: 'The subject intrigued me. They're real bees, they really do exist. I saw some of them. They're vicious bastards, the result of a cross-strain from Africa and Brazil. And it was certainly one of the weirdest films I've ever been on — all of us going around in protective headgear and clothing, dressed in different colours so you could distinguish who people were. The director was in red. Mine was white.

'They used three kinds of bees for effects: real killer bees in close-up. Smaller drones without stings for long-shot. And artificial bees they'd blow at you through a wind machine to simulate an attack! The miracle is that I got through it without being stung — because a lot of people were.'

To show there were no hard feelings, Caine signed on again for Allen — this time aboard a sunken ship in the Pacific in a sequel to the hugely successful *Poseidon Adventure*. He played the skipper of a run-down salvage vessel that reaches the huge upturned hull of the Poseidon, still gamely afloat with its cargo of corpses, and cuts through the steel doors and myriad passages to claim the deceased passengers' valuables from the strong-room as treasure-trove. *Beyond the Poseidon Adventure* was filmed off Catalina Island south of Malibu. 'I had to learn to scuba dive in the freezing Pacific,' Caine recalls. 'I've always suffered from claustrophobia, and never thought

80

I could do it. But in this business, you learn fast.' Another $1 million in his own strong-room didn't hurt, either.

In Hollywood they call it a 'snuff movie', where actors really do suffer. Soaked to the skin, blackened by smoke, bruised and battered, choked by fumes, it was no picnic at sea. With one accord the critics leaped on the film with unconcealed delight, and tore it to shreds. The *What's On in London* critic summed up: 'Beyond Poseidon, beyond logic, beyond me'.

Oh dear. But Michael Caine kept a straight face and his smile intact and said phlegmatically: 'Critics are a funny lot. If you always play the same kind of character they say you're typecast. If you experiment as I do, they ask why you don't stick to the parts you know'.

By now he had come to another watershed in his life, and made a decision that was to affect him for years to come: to give up England, and make his career in Hollywood. Britain, with its decreasing social values, union unrest and crushing tax penalties, had lost its charm for him. The seductive sunshine of California, the leisurely social pace, the friends he had made, beckoned.

Finally he had come to terms with his future, and with himself. For years the financial pressures had been weighing on him. Agents' percentages, lawyers' fees, the whole expensive life-style he had accrued and wanted to retain, all made only one decision possible for him: he emigrated.

Caine tells the story of the last straw that decided him. It took less than twenty seconds, and it happened when he called in a nineteen-year-old junior electrician to rewire one of the rooms at the Mill House. The youth stared around open-mouthed — and refused point-blank to do the work. When Caine demanded to know why, the other replied: 'No-one should have all this!' And left.

Caine, considerably shaken, said later: 'It not only upset me, it terrified me. He wasn't even an old man. He had all his life in front of him. People shouldn't be surprised that I 'left — they should be astonished that I stayed so long. I paid my dues, hundreds of thousands of pounds in taxes. Why should I apologise to anyone?'

He sold the Mill House in 1979 to rock guitarist Jimmy Page of the Led Zeppelin group. The price was £650,000. Michael and Shakira and Natasha Caine moved to Hollywood, to the Big Orange state of California, rented houses for four years, and finally achieved the

Another spectacular — Beyond the Poseidon Adventure — *directed by Irwin Allen. Known in the trade as a 'snuff' movie. Caine, Sally Field, Karl Malden.*

Both Michael Caine and Maggie Smith, who won an Oscar, were in sparkling form in Neil Simon's California Suite.

82

home they wanted — a luxury bungalow on a hilltop in Beverly Hills above the smog belt, with a view of the whole city. But they left with a heavy heart, reluctant exiles.

A complete change of pace came with *California Suite,* adapted by millionaire playwright Neil Simon from his Broadway hit. It was a series of four playlets, and Caine's segment starred him opposite Maggie Smith, playing the husband of an Oscar-nominated actress who accuses him of sexual ambidexterity. Caine was in sparkling form, and was the first to congratulate his co-star when she won the real Oscar for her performance. It remains one of his favourite films.

No-one could say that Michael Caine was typecast any more. The laconic Cockney anti-hero from Alfie and Harry Palmer days had become swallowed up in such a variety of roles that it was impossible to pin him down into any one character. The voice was still immediately recognisable, that was all, a gift for impersonators from Peter Sellers downwards to employ and enjoy.

Now here he was on the high seas around Antigua in a pirate pot-boiler called *The Island,* from Peter Benchley, who wrote *Jaws.* It was an unpleasant folk tale in which Michael played an investigative reporter whose son (Jeffrey Frank) is kidnapped by a group of brigands from the old Captain Morgan days, a garish band of cut-throats led by Dudley Sutton in a grotesque uniform of high boots and jock-strap more suited to a Soho sex club. They slaughter tourists and create a Bermuda Triangle mystery at the centre of the theme.

Caine remembers fourteen weeks of blistering sun afloat in shark-infested waters, with a humid, oppressive atmosphere pervading the unit. The director, Michael Ritchie, tried to comfort him. 'When was the last time you heard of a movie star being eaten by a shark?' he inquired.

'I'm not worried about the last time,' Caine retorted. 'I'm worried about the first time. I'm not about to be the first movie star to be eaten by a shark.'

He remained intact, and so did his professional career — the critics slated the movie but let Michael off with a caution. Close call, though. The influential Dilys Powell in London's *Punch* magazine acidly commented: 'Disturbing to find this sanguinary tosh is directed by the gifted Michael Ritchie'.

There was a lot more blood spilled on screen in his next film, a psychological thriller called *Dressed to Kill*. It was a study in horror directed by Brian de Palma, then rapidly making his name in that genre and hoping to be hailed as a new Alfred Hitchcock.

Caine played a psychiatrist involved with Angie Dickinson until she is slashed to death in a lift by a transvestite maniac wielding a cut-throat razor. Somewhere in New York there's a psychotic killer dressed in drag and a blonde wig stalking the wet streets in search of prey. Nasty stuff, and there was a great deal of controversy over the explicit butchery. The result: it grossed $40 m. world-wide, and became the most successful picture Caine had ever made.

'I'd never done that kind of real heavy thriller before,' Caine says. 'I knew it was a risk — but it could work. I didn't worry about what people would think: as an actor you have to go ahead and do things you've never done before. But it was a very strange role to play.'

He has his own answer to those who became disturbed at the number of cheapie pictures depicting wanton violence on women that were filtering in from America, and linking this one with them. 'How many films did Jack the Ripper see? The whole of movies and drama is about people in jeopardy. Even comedy is jeopardy sometimes. This was a study of a schizophrenic, which is what interested me about it.'

Unexpectedly, after this dark labyrinth of terror, Michael Caine went straight into another nightmare thriller called *The Hand*. He sums it up: 'Very strong stuff, about a painter who loses a hand in a car accident, and the hand comes back and starts killing people!' Shades of Edgar Allan Poe — but without the quality. It was so bad it wasn't seen for four years, and then only slipped into fringe cinemas. Caine prefers to forget it.

With *Escape to Victory*, however, he was back into the main stream, a major international film directed by John Huston and starring established figures like Max von Sydow and Sylvester Stallone taking time off from the *Rocky* trilogy. It was a kind of 'Colditz Story' set on a soccer pitch, with a prisoner-of-war squad using a match with the German national team as a cover for a daring escape. To help the publicity, genuine footballers headed by Pelé and Osvaldo Ardiles were hired to boot the ball around on location in Budapest and add soccer quality, at least, to a saga that failed to match up to its potential.

'Michael was exactly the limey we wanted,' Huston declared. 'Smart and resourceful. I chose him personally. Besides, he knows more about the game than I do!' In fact Caine explained the finer points of the game to an equally bewildered 'Sly' Stallone, who during filming managed to crack three ribs in goal against a hard drive from the opposition. 'That's the way he is,' says Michael. 'Three ribs he regarded as small beer.'

Two more films he had under his own belt were *Ashanti*, a routine chase thriller set in East Africa with William Holden and Peter Ustinov ('I loathed every second of it'); and a wild comedy called *Harry and Walter Go to New York*, directed by Mark Rydell, in which he played a safe-cracker.

But now, in 1981, came a film that was startlingly close to *Sleuth* in its intricacies and intrigue, *Death Trap*. Ira Levin's edge-of-the-seat murder thriller had filled theatres in the West End and on Broadway. Now it was skilfully turned into a gripping film by director Sidney Lumet, with the apparently odd casting of Christopher (*Superman*) Reeve and sexy Dyan Cannon in a fresh battle of wits with playwright Caine, smarting from an opening-night flop. It was well received, and added another acting scalp to Michael Caine's belt.

Chapter 9
'All I ever wanted'

People were murmuring about an Oscar nomination for *Death Trap*, but Michael Caine did not stop to wait for the mail man. The nomination never came, anyway. Instead he moved smartly across the Atlantic yet again — not to Britain, but to Eire.

In common with other star tax exiles like Roger Moore, Sean Connery and Dudley Moore, he had grown somewhat sensitive about setting foot on English soil knowing he was allowed only ninety days a year before the Inland Revenue sent in the hounds.

But in Dublin, amid the cobbled streets and the historic University buildings, he was able to take on a role which had emanated from another West End play hit, and make it something special. *Educating Rita* was about a working-class girl with aspirations of intellectual grandeur who sets out to better herself through education. Rita, delightfully played by Julie Walters, is a humble hairdresser's assistant with brains who persuades a world-weary tutor, alcoholic and melancholic, to help her attain the English degree she hungers after.

For the teacher it is more like third-degree as the barriers of self-revelation tumble down. Like Professor Higgins in *Pygmalion*, he finds himself irresistibly drawn to his protégée. Caine, overweight, teetering gently among his books and the hidden bottle on the shelves, produced a performance that for the first time drew tears of real emotion and empathy from audiences everywhere. Julie had already won deserved praise from the stage. Under Lewis Gilbert's sensitive direction she transferred her biting, voluble, yet eventually vulnerable portrayal to the screen with authority and apparent ease.

Julie Walters, as Rita, being educated by Michael Caine.

The Jigsaw Man, *with Laurence Olivier.*

87

Caine, far from being eclipsed, matched her decibel for decibel, from jaundiced acerbity to tender understanding. He won his third Academy Award nomination for it. 'It was a part,' he said, 'that I could really get my teeth into, a marvellous part, the kind an actor dreams about.' He was pleased as Punch that Gilbert had coaxed new depths from him, sixteen long years after they were first teamed on *Alfie*.

When the curtains finally parted at the Los Angeles Music Centre on Oscar night almost a year later, the entire British contingent in Hollywood, and a few more besides, were rooting for him. Sadly, it was third time unlucky. Robert Duvall won the American vote for *Tender Mercies*.

Afterwards Caine consoled himself: 'I already knew in my heart that I wouldn't get it. Nobody told me, because the Oscars are completely honest. But I had a faint inkling that it wasn't going to be my night. Let me put it this way: you don't win the Oscar or *lose* it — you win it or you don't win it, so there's no loss. Being nominated is important. Winning is very, very important. Your price has already gone up because you were nominated. It goes up 50 per cent. If you win, it goes up by 100 per cent!' But with his casual honesty, he adds: 'I'd love to win it. It would be wonderful. And one day I will, I'm sure. . .'

Caine has been around long enough to know that it is not worth reaching for the pills if you don't get Hollywood's ultimate accolade. 'I'm phlegmatic about the whole thing. The Oscars, Hollywood. Afterwards, with the cards, bottles of champagne, flowers and boxes of chocolates that came to the house, you'd have thought I'd won it! I went to a party later and got a standing ovation.' Sympathy vote? Not at-all. Michael Caine's still a winner, and both he and the world know it.

Meantime he had made *The Honorary Consul*, from Graham Greene's novel about Our Man in a forgotten country, drinking too much (again for Michael), more dipso than diplo, on the skids both in his job and in his personal life. His routine is altered alarmingly when he is kidnapped by political extremists and held to ransom in a squalid shack in a shanty town, thereby becoming an unwilling pawn in the diplomatic game, less immune than he realised. Richard Gere was brought in for the raunchy American box-office, starring as a virile young doctor who tries to help the hapless consul. At

Shepperton Studios where they filmed the interiors, Gere would sit alone in the bustling restaurant at lunchtime, an island of isolation in his own 'space'. No-one approached him. Nobody, except Caine, even said even 'Hi!' And that was usually just a nod and a word.

Michael, that most gregarious of characters, looked across one day from his sociable, noisy table, and wondered aloud: 'That guy is very difficult to get to know. I think it's because he takes himself so seriously'. The pair seemed as far apart as the two polar caps, and maybe it reflected on the screen: the hoped-for 'explosive' chemistry turned into the traditional damp squib. Nice idea. Better lunch next time.

Next time took Michael rolling down to Rio for a sexy — rather than a sex — comedy called, symbolically as it turned out, *Blame it on Rio*. It was directed by the experienced Stanley Donen, a man with an excellent track record for sophisticated comedy. Only this time something went wrong.

Blame it on the theme? The story revolved around Caine, on holiday in glamorous Rio with his best friend (Joseph Bologna) who is seduced by the teenage daughter (Michelle Johnson) of the said friend. Caine then has to go through the whole charade of helping his aggrieved chum track down the villain who done her wrong, i.e. himself.

Feminists throughout America rose en masse to denounce: the film, Caine, the director, the girl, the whole concept. The critics were not too happy, either, though in Europe they were more charitable and the film made enough at the box-office to satisfy the backers.

Caine had learned another lesson, a trifle late in life: 'I knew it was a bit dodgy, but I went into it with my eyes open. It hadn't occurred to me that there might be problems. I'd seen nothing in the feminist press except articles about how wonderful it was for all these older women to be going out with young boys. So I thought: well, maybe they won't be hypocritical. But I made a bad mistake. Still, hypocrisy abounds in the United States. It's such a hypocritical society in many ways. At least it didn't do my image any harm. In fact, it's done me a lot of good. I was trying to prove I could play comedy, and I did. The thing they attacked was the taste.'

The film's title in the US was *Love Rio*. If the local critics and the feminists did not, at least it grossed $35 million in the States. It also launched Michelle Johnson, a girl with legs that began at her

Michael and Shakira Caine, and their daughter Natasha.

shoulder-blades, into the mid-1980s with a vengeance. Michael Caine wished her luck and went on his way. . . to the Caribbean.

There, on the island of St Lucia, he found himself among the tropical fauna and flora of a way-out comedy called, simply, *Water*. His co-star was the Glaswegian comic Billy Connolly. Caine's role: the governor of the island, a small, insignificant British possession conveniently forgotten by both time and the Foreign Office. . . until the dreaded oil is discovered and it's up for grabs.

Michael sports a natty blazer and flannels, with an accent to match. Shades of Lieutenant Gonville Bromhead in *Zulu*. 'The guy is crazy, but lovable,' he says. 'That's what I liked about him. He has his own sense of honour, but basically events just run him down like a steam-roller.'

The wild and hairy Connolly, like a heathen Che Guevara, plays a local revolutionary who has taken a vow never to speak — so he sings his political sermons in thick Glasgow accents reminiscent of a bad Saturday night in Sauchiehall Street. Almost inevitably, the extraordinary casting came up trumps. Michael and Billy hit it off on the spot and became firm friends, two honest blokes adrift in a sea of shark-infested superficiality, in a here-today-gone-tomorrow business they both had known and conquered.

'Michael is a real person,' Billy would tell you. 'He's honest, down-to-earth, and genuinely funny.' High praise from a professional comic. But then, it takes one to know one.

Michael enjoyed the location, the script, the role and the company. It was like a breath of fresh air to be among a group of young, creative film-makers working to a modest budget. George Harrison, the ex-Beatle, was one of the producers. Dick Clement, co-scripter of *The Likely Lads*, was the director. In St Lucia and on the English location in Hartland Point, Devon, they would sit and talk and laugh and exchange lurid stories until the early hours. . . and be there, spot on call, soon after dawn next day.

With his batteries recharged, Caine went back into the murky spy business. By now a film that had broken down like a carthorse in mid-stride was back in business: *The Jigsaw Man*, in which he once again found himself in illustrious company — Laurence Olivier co-starred in the story loosely based on the Kim Philby espionage case. The money had run out with a week to go, and the director, Terence Young, had been forced to close up the shop. Everyone grew

Shangri-La. The Caines relax at their home in the Hollywood hills 'above the smog level'. Thirty years a loser, but now twenty years a winner.

nine months older, then came back into harness, and the movie was completed, and ready to be released. Young was very happy with the result: 'Michael and Larry are absolutely right for it. I couldn't ask for two more professional people,' he said.

After *Water*, it was another spy thriller *The Holcroft Covenant* that took Caine to Munich, to strap on a holster and get ready to duck. Once again, Michael is up to his neck in suspense and intrigue in a fast-paced thriller directed by John Frankenheimer, with Victoria Tennant providing the glamour and Michael Lonsdale (from *Day of the Jackal*) and Anthony Andrews keeping the guessing game going.

And so, today, thirty losing years and twenty winning ones on, Michael Caine is rich and running. He is a popular figure in Hollywood, where they rate achievement above all else. Michael and Shakira are at the top of the Beverly Hills social register, invited to endless parties and charity functions, but mostly preferring to spend their leisure time with people they know in their own homes.

Caine's own home is his base, and his pride and joy. A rambling farmhouse-style bungalow, it is set high above the smog belt beyond Benedict Canyon, white-washed into shimmering brilliance in the California sunshine. He paid $1 million for it when he bought it in 1970 from Lance Reventlow, son of Woolworth heiress Barbara Hutton, since when it has quadrupled in value.

Now he sits on his lawn by the pool, surrounded by the greenery and rockeries he has tended himself, musing on his fortunes, on fame, on fate, and on the way he challenged and beat the system.

'Funny thing,' he says. 'When I was poor, people used to say: "If you ever become rich, boy, money won't make you happy". But it has. I have a great deal of money, and I'm perfectly happy. I have all I ever wanted: to become a millionaire, to be a big film star, to become the best actor I possibly could be. I have no inhibitions and no hang-ups.'

Except, maybe, just one. The future. Michael Caine studies the glowing end of his Havana cigar, and ponders for a moment. Then he says: 'People also say to me: *Do you get homesick?*'

'*I don't get* homesick. The homesickness is constant. It's just an ache. It's like having a sore toe. I try to forget about it, but really I only forget it when I go to sleep. Soon, I think, I've got to come home. . .'

And, sooner or later, he would.

The Films of Michael Caine

A HILL IN KOREA, 1956, directed by *Julian Amyes*

HOW TO MURDER A RICH UNCLE, 1957, directed by *Nigel Patrick*

THE KEY, 1958, directed by *Carol Reed*

BLIND SPOT, 1958, directed by *Peter Maxwell*

THE TWO-HEADED SPY, 1958, directed by *André de Toth*

FOXHOLE IN CAIRO, 1960, directed by *John Moxey*

THE BULLDOG BREED, 1960, directed by *Robert Asher*

THE DAY THE EARTH CAUGHT FIRE, 1961, directed by *Val Guest*

SOLO FOR SPARROW, 1962, directed by *Gordon Flemyng*

THE WRONG ARM OF THE LAW, 1962, directed by *Cliff Owen*

ZULU, 1963, directed by *Cy Endfield*

THE IPCRESS FILE, 1965, directed by *Sidney J. Furie*

ALFIE, 1966, directed by *Lewis Gilbert*

THE WRONG BOX, 1966, directed by *Bryan Forbes*

GAMBIT, 1966, directed by *Ronald Neame*

FUNERAL IN BERLIN, 1966, directed by *Guy Hamilton*

HURRY SUNDOWN, 1966, directed by *Otto Preminger*

BILLION DOLLAR BRAIN, 1967, directed by *Ken Russell*

WOMAN TIMES SEVEN, 1967, directed by *Vittorio de Sica*

DEADFALL, 1968, directed by *Bryan Forbes*

PLAY DIRTY, 1968, directed by *André de Toth*

THE MAGUS, 1968, directed by *Guy Green*

THE ITALIAN JOB, 1969, directed by *Peter Collinson*

THE BATTLE OF BRITAIN, 1969, directed by *Guy Hamilton*

TOO LATE THE HERO, 1969, directed by *Robert Aldrich*

THE LAST VALLEY, 1970, directed by *James Clavell*

GET CARTER, 1970, directed by *Michael Hodges*

KIDNAPPED, 1971, directed by *Delbert Mann*

ZEE AND CO, 1971, directed by *Brian G. Hutton*

PULP, 1972, directed by *Michael Hodges*

SLEUTH, 1972, directed by *Joseph L. Mankiewicz*

THE BLACK WINDMILL, 1974, directed by *Don Siegel*

THE MARSEILLES CONTRACT, 1974, directed by *Robert Parrish*

THE WILBY CONSPIRACY, 1975, directed by *Ralph Nelson*

THE ROMANTIC ENGLISHWOMAN, 1975, directed by *Joseph Losey*

PEEPER, 1976, directed by *Peter Hyams*

THE MAN WHO WOULD BE KING, 1976, directed by *John Huston*

THE SILVER BEARS, 1976, directed by *Ivan Passer*

THE EAGLE HAS LANDED, 1976, directed by *John Sturges*

A BRIDGE TOO FAR, 1976, directed by *Richard Attenborough*

HARRY AND WALTER GO TO NEW YORK, 1976, directed by *Mark Rydell*

BEYOND THE POSEIDON ADVENTURE, 1977, directed by *Irwin Allen*

CALIFORNIA SUITE, 1978, directed by *Herbert Ross*

ASHANTI, 1978, directed by *Richard Fleischer*

THE ISLAND, 1978, directed by *Michael Ritchie*

THE SWARM, 1979, directed by *Irwin Allen*

DRESSED TO KILL, 1980, directed by *Brian de Palma*

ESCAPE TO VICTORY, 1981, directed by *John Huston*

THE HAND, 1982, directed by *Oliver Stone*

DEATH TRAP, 1982, directed by *Sidney Lumet*

EDUCATING RITA, 1983, directed by *Lewis Gilbert*

THE JIGSAW MAN, 1983, directed by *Terence Young*

THE HONORARY CONSUL, 1983, directed by *John MacKenzie*

BLAME IT ON RIO, 1983, directed by *Stanley Donen*

WATER, 1984, directed by *Dick Clement*

THE HOLCROFT COVENANT, 1985, directed by *John Frankenheimer*